Sheffield's Pubs

Last Orders

by

Douglas Lamb

Author of

'A Pub on Every Corner'

last orders

Text copyright 2000 © Douglas Lamb
Photographic copyright 2000 © Douglas Lamb and Stephen J Reaney

ISBN 0 9534267 2 6

First published in 2000 by Pickard Publishing

The right of Douglas Lamb to be identified as author of this work
has been asserted by him in accordance with the
Copyright, Design and Patent Act 1988.

Published and Printed by Pickard Publishing
Unit 11 • Riverside Park • Sheaf Gardens • Sheffield S2 4BB
Telephone 0114 275 7222 or 275 7444
e.mail: Pickards@btinternet.com

last orders

Contents

last orders

I should like to thank Stephen J Reaney
for once again helping with the photographic work
connected with this book.

My thanks also to all the kind people who have
allowed me to use their photographs;
to those who have shared with me their wisdom and
who have told me their stories and, of course,
to the staff of the Local Studies Section, Sheffield Central Library,
who have once again guided me towards the
paths which lead to true enlightenment.

Special thanks to Pam Radford, David English, Malcolm Nunn,
Ray Dyson, Julie Siddons, Cyril Slinn, Doug Sanderson,
Joe Castle, Doreen Mieszczak, Diane Gascoyne, Jack Ambler,
Thelma Coy, Len Widdowson, Linda Hutton, (CAMRA),
Chris Pickard and Mick Liversidge.

Authors Notes

Well I never! Here I am in a position that I swore I would never again find myself - about to write an introduction to a book on pubs!

When I finally managed, after almost four years of enjoyable, but gruelling work, to get "A Pub On Every Corner" on to the shelves of the bookshops, I mentally slumped back, exhausted, but satisfied. It was done and as such I foolishly thought that I could then, at last, leave these important, fascinating, but time consuming establishments behind me and head off in a completely new direction - been there, done that, written the book. That sort of thing. It was, alas, not to be. Not by a long chalk.

I have done various things since then, even written another book about a completely different subject, but well over three years since "the pub book" was published, I have come to realise that, for better or worse, I am stuck with pubs; I have created something that will dog my footsteps and stand in my shadow all the way to the grave and perhaps beyond! I have become, in this short time, known to many as The Pub Man!

I don't really mind this, of course. A small measure of fame, no matter how fleeting, has spiced up my drab life no end, now that I have become accustomed to strange men accosting me in libraries in order to ask me obscure and difficult questions, the answers to which I usually haven't the faintest idea. I have very quickly become skilled in the noble art of generalisation and deviation. This is known in politics as the "I'm glad you asked me that" defence - otherwise known as flannelling!

All this continuing attention and the variety of questions asked me gave me food for thought; a reason to examine the book and its contents. From these musings has emerged the realisation that I need once again to drag out the aged typewriter (no computer science for me, pal!), sit down and do battle once again in the cause of pubs. (Actually since I began writing this book I have joined the cutting edge of technology and aquired something that I believe is called a computer)

Why? The answer is simple. I considered that the first book was large, but it obviously wasn't large enough. It left out too much information; it left gaps. It covered an area which was, for the sensible reasons that I explained in the book, mostly confined to the centre of Sheffield, plus some coverage of suburbs like Crookes, Handsworth, Attercliffe and Burngreave. More was therefore needed.

Having realised this, I intend in this second book to fill in some of the gaps and plug some of the holes. This will obviously increase the amount of information available, but will it staunch the flow of questions? I doubt it. But that's okay. If people want to ask me questions, I don't really mind trying to answer them. Like I said, a little fame is always welcome!

How much new information does this book contain? That's easily answered. To attempt to list every pub in the Sheffield area that I didn't cover before, both old and new, would be a fair sized job - a daunting and very probably a nigh on impossible task. That is why I haven't even attempted to do this. What I have tried to do is gather together a further collection of pubs from areas surrounding the city. It isn't complete and I have no doubt that I have missed out pubs here and there in various villages. I have also no doubt that at least one person, and if I am lucky, only one, will notice this or that omission and point it out to me at the earliest opportunity - usually loudly and at an embarrassing moment!

The best example of this "pointing out" was a man in Melbourne, Australia, where ever that is, who wrote to me and who took me to task in no uncertain terms for failing to include in the first book, The Penny Black, that grimly modern and soulless pub built into the corner of the Royal Mail sorting office on Pond Street. There was, of course, no stamped addressed envelope with his badly spelt letter, which is probably why he didn't receive an answer. Struggling authors don't write to places like Australia. At least this one doesn't!

I had, in fact, mentioned early in the book, obviously in a section that he hadn't bothered to read, "Old Buildings, New Pubs", that establishments such as The Penny Black wouldn't be included in the text due entirely to the fact that they were far too new and were almost entirely devoid of any historical interest. This wasn't the only pub that I excluded, there were a couple of dozen more.

As I have just written, this book will be mostly about the villages on the outskirts of Sheffield - those previously independent little communities who, before submitting to the slow but certain encroachment of the city, once led their own lives, at their own pace and who nourished their own special and precious customs and habits.

Many of these places, once the foundation blocks of the agricultural system which underpinned the backbone of England, still struggle to maintain a separate identity with varying levels of success. Rightly, they are proud of their histories, remember the heroes whose names are carved on the village war memorial, support a parish church and perhaps a chapel or two. They run a football team, perhaps one which plays cricket as well, and strive to be, each in their own individual way, just that little bit different from "them dahnt road"! More power to them all. Individuals are becoming scarce these days. If I can, by grouping together the local pubs in each of these villages, help them to still feel valid, then so be it. I shall be delighted.

Many of the pubs in the villages were taken by discharged soldiers or disabled men who could no longer work in their previous employment. It was no problem for them to be given a licence and it was, as far as The Authorities were concerned, a good idea. In the case of the soldiers, it was a substitute for the pension they never received for serving their country, perhaps in the Napoleonic Wars; in the case of the disabled men, it kept them out of the village workhouse and stopped them from becoming a drain on the parish purse. Although mostly in the areas of England which boast a naval tradition, many either disabled or retired sailors, especially those who had served at the end of the 18th or the beginning of the 19th centuries, put enough prize money aside - a couple of hundred pounds would have been enough - and opened a country ale-house. Remember Treasure Island?

I think it is very likely that the village pubs and outlying country pubs, which form most of this book, will often date back as far as the 17th or even 16th centuries. I also think that, at least at the outset, most of them would have only held an ale- or beer-house licence. When dating these pubs, however, I have erred on the side of caution and only given a date about which I am reasonably certain. In my previous book, I made a point which I will repeat here. It is extremely difficult, in fact verging on the impossible, to accurately date when a pub opened and also the dates on which a landlord either came or went. Because of this, there will be many descriptions of pubs which contain the words "possibly" or "probably". I make no apologies for this vagueness. I would prefer to appear vague about a date than make a positive statement of fact which later proves to be wrong. There will no doubt be enough mistakes in this book without that as well!

I have made use of trade directories, as many historians do, which tell the date when a landlord was there, but not when he either came or went - the duration of his tenure. Some pubs I have traced from 1825 up to the middle of or the late 19th century. If any reader would like to carry out further research on a particular pub or group of pubs, say in one village, then the directories are all there in the local history section of the Central Library. You may well find that a visit is both interesting and rewarding.

Please don't expect miracles. I haven't been able, in many cases, to find an interesting story, or small piece of history, to pin to the pubs that I have included for the simple reason that there isn't anything like that in their backgrounds. They are, when the chips are down, just pubs. Some, indeed most of them, may be old and as such they probably appear as if they should be fairly bursting with historical goodies. Unfortunately this is not usually the case. They are just old pubs, nothing much more. To compensate for this sometimes thin level of interest regarding the pubs, I have added where possible little snippets of information about the villages that they grace and the people who lived there.

This hasn't always been easy. In my deepest depressions, when I am struggling to lay by the heels the tiny, but elusive fragments of information that we all like to read about, I have often nurtured very unkind thoughts about those forefathers of ours for not having had the gumption to leave better, or in many cases, any records of events which happened one, two or three centuries ago.

For example, how many of you have a sepia photograph of some dead relative that no-one in the family can put a name to - Aunt Doreen could have done, but she died last year - although they may only have only died a couple of generations ago? All because nobody thought to put a name and date on the back of the card. I've a dozen or more. They are, historically speaking, not long dead, but they will most likely remain forever a mystery.

In between the villages which surround Sheffield are the infill housing developments. These have gradually formed links between the villages and blurred the once distinct boundaries of each little territorial area. As the houses were built so were the shops, the schools and the pubs. I don't, for the most part, intend to mention many of these "new" pubs. Some I shall do especially if they have, in their relatively short lives, gathered any history around themselves, if only perhaps in the name. A good example of this is **The Shiny Sheff** in Lodgemoor. The name commemorates Sheffield's own battleship. It is important to include it.

There are a number of pubs which are lonely places, separated from any village. These were usually built, many years ago, to serve a turnpike or a tiny agricultural hamlet now gone. These are some of the oldest pubs that I have covered here and some of the best. Most of them have at least a few lines of history behind them, some a lot more than that. I have included these places in the chapter covering the village nearest to them.

There is, you will find, another section of this book that by concentrating on a different type of pub wanders away from the true path of recording old pubs. I actually included a few examples of them in the first book, but only at the end and then as an afterthought.

These are the new pubs which have been created in old buildings. Or to put it another way, in buildings which were built some time ago for other purposes than for the sale of strong drink. There are a surprising and growing number of these and to investigate them I must mostly return to the city centre because this is, as a general rule, where they are.

Perhaps, for these new/old places, the title of "pub" is too simple a name. It is probably better that I have decided to attempt to refer to them by their various and, to my English ears, faintly alien titles - wine bars, restaurant bars, cafe bars, trattorias, brasseries - these sort of names. All of them, call them what you will, everybody else does, have been expensively, and in most cases, tastefully refurbished and are almost unrecognisable from their previous incarnations. Bank premises, a post office, a fire station, a building society offices, various shops, a public baths and a steel works are just a sample of these buildings now cosily sheltering and entertaining drinkers and diners.

All are a welcome addition to the city's licenced premises, but also all are far removed from that elusive and possibly only illusory entity, the Traditional English Pub! I like them! They are clean and warm and inviting; the food is usually good, the service excellent and the beer cold. They are a pleasant and comfortable change in direction from the appalling attempts made by the brewery giants in the late 70's and early 80's to alter what was already there. This was achieved by cheap and tacky facelifts made to cater for the latest perceived fad or fashion. Or nasty and equally cheap modernisation work which robbed old pubs of all the character built up through the passage of time, in a desperate bid to snatch custom from the place next door. Does success in big business really mean that all vestiges of good taste and discernment must be thrown out of the window? It appears so. Fortunately, while some of these appalling pubs remain, the new/old pubs appearing are far better and I feel that this must be the adopted way in the future. It needs to be, for drink is no longer cheap and customers who pay the modern prices demand a decent place in which to consume it. The elderly and middle-aged may accept the old ways, but the generation up and coming, who were brought up to expect a better standard of living, will not.

This, coupled with the vastly improved, and almost sensible, licencing laws and "permitted hours" in this country, can only be for the better. Who knows, perhaps in time we may even get used to drinking in a pub named **The Ferret & Trouserleg!**

I'm sure that the young people have already. Mentioning the new name of this pub, once very reasonably known as The Gladstone, brings me to one of the most annoying trends, at least to me, which has become more prevalent in recent years. This has been the need that the brewers and the pub owning companies seem to have to change pub names from something old and dignified to something modern and jokey.

The former Gladstone

It is easy, as a middle aged man, to be labelled an old fogy or a stick-in-the-mud and I won't deny that on this subject I may well be either or both. However, while I accept that the pub business is becoming more and more difficult to make profitable for sundry reasons, I cannot honestly see how changing, for example, the once logically named Woodseats Hotel to **The Floozy & Firkin** can do very much for the pub's profitability. Actually, I discovered recently that this pub has now reverted to its original name. Shall I rest my case?

I suppose that plenty of people will hold directly opposite views to myself regarding pub names and will readily accept these changes as part of that mystical thing called progress. I'm prepared to bet that most of these are much younger and have more flexible minds than I have. I have grown up with pubs called The King's Head and The Red Lion and I am comfortable with these names. They are part of the England that I know and understand. They have some history and interest behind them. What history is there behind such a name as The Fitzooth & Firkin?

The Fitzooth & Firkin
formerly the Nottingham House

Anyway, enough of this. I know that I ramble on. Forgive me, I mean well. Why not read this book and enjoy it.

The Foundry & Firkin formerly the Bee Hive

CHAPTER ONE
SOME SHEFFIELD BREWERIES

Starting to write a book, line one, chapter one and going on from there is always difficult. It needs a kick start; it needs a subject of interest, something that the readers can enjoy from the very outset and perhaps think about. I pondered on this and decided to go right back to the very grass roots of the subject. I realised that in a book about pubs, I had to start with that most vital of public houses necessities - beer. Hence this chapter about breweries. Or rather, three old Sheffield breweries.

A public house, be it called an inn, a tavern, an hotel or whatever, has one thing in common with its peers - it sells beer. Of course, as this is a history book, I am writing mostly about "the olden days". Today there are plenty of establishments, known loosely as pubs, which make a very good living without huge sales of this once considered essential commodity and who base their sales on wines, spirits and various fairly noxious fluids, brightly coloured and usually drunk straight from the bottle. These places, in my opinion, aren't proper pubs; not like the pubs that I knew and it is quite possible that the owners would be appalled to be even so considered.

A pub, rooting back through my memory to when I first remember them, was a place where draught beer ruled the roost and this precious fluid was usually served directly from the pump into a straight glass - with a half for the missus! Landlords' reputations were made or broken by the quality of their draught beer.

For pubs to thrive, breweries were vital and local breweries were as much a part of a town as the church or the town hall. Beer in these places was brewed on the premises, using local water, then sealed in barrels and bottles and delivered to the pubs in the surrounding area.

That was a local brewery and here in Sheffield, especially during the later half of the 19th century, there was a great many. Alas, no longer.

The Kelham Island Brewery

It is unfortunate that as the 21st century arrives, in Sheffield local breweries are becoming not just scarce but non-existent. Here, I mean breweries which had the capacity to supply large numbers of pubs, most of which they owned. There are, now that the brewing climate has radically altered in Sheffield, several small breweries which supply a tiny number of local pubs.

The best known, the oldest and the largest of these is The Kelham Island Brewery, Alma Street. This operates from its new building in front of the industrial museum and is owned by the same company which owns The Fat Cat pub which is beside it.

Although it is, to all intents and purposes, a very small brewery, ironically it is now the largest brewery in Sheffield. Since it was built, it has slowly increased the number of pubs that it supplies with beer. Recently, this list was increased by the inclusion of The Ranmoor Inn, Fulwood Road, The Plough, Sandygate Road, The Old Grindstone, Crookes and The Millhouses, Abbeydale Road. These four public houses are now part of the Sheffield Pub Company.

Among the beers produced in Alma Street are Steel City, Kelham Gold and Kelham Island Bitter - which was in the top six, in its category, in August this year in the CAMRA Awards at the Great British Beer Festival, which is held annually at London's Olympia.

The Abbeydale Brewery, Aizlewood Road is, I believe, run by a former brewer from Kelham Island Brewery, Pat Morton. It produces a range of about eight beers with strengths ranging from 3.6% to a hefty 11%.

Not in Sheffield, but only just outside in a building, which is part of the Wentworth Woodhouse estate, The Powerhouse, Gun Park, Wentworth is the Wentworth Brewery. It is only about a year old and has a connection with the Commerical, Station Road, Chapeltown. It brews several popular beers. The head brewer is Gary Sheriff.

Finally, there is a brewery behind the Frog and Parrot, Division Street. It brews beer mainly for consumption in its own pub. These are incredibly strong "barley wine" type beers. It is scorned by CAMRA though, as apparently it brews using malt extract and this, it seems, is beyond the pale.

There have been a couple of other breweries, which are no longer in business - Drummond's Brewery, Heeley Road and a brewery attached to the Foundry & Firkin, West Street. It used to supply the pubs in the Firkin group, but closed when the group was sold by Punch Taverns.

Finally, the former Wellington, now the Cask & Cutler, situated on the corner of Henry Street and Infirmary Road, appears to have everything a brewery needs except for assembling the requisite equipment. This, I believe, is one for the future.

Breweries, I always think, are like fish - the big ones eat the smaller ones until all that is left is a tiny, but powerful group of even bigger ones. It may be a simplistic view, but I feel that it is about right. There is, to be frank, no place in modern business for the small, local brewery. It is all a question of economics. Size cuts costs. The multi-labelling of products - beer is after all that - where one beer is called a different name from the same beer sold in another area is common practice. This means that the actual brewing process is larger, but being in the same place, is simpler and cheaper. This centralisation of production allows one large brewing combine to cover a huge area. In some cases larger than the British Isles. It is not difficult, nowadays, to enjoy a pint of Tetley's in Benidorm!

While this obviously makes good business sense to the accountants, it does little or nothing to save the local breweries. Their attitude isn't surprising. These breweries no longer fit in; the concept is old fashioned and so the smaller concerns are bought out, stripped of their assets and allowed to perish or to become a mere bottling or cask washing plant. It has happened too many times in Sheffield not to be true. The drinking public has aided and abetted this situation by its passive acceptance, although it is difficult to see what they could have done.

The generations born during the last couple of centuries knew nothing about fancy packaging, the fads and fancies of the day or ice cold lager beer with strange sounding foreign names. It just didn't happen then. The choice was limited, especially for the working man who was, at these times, the lifeblood of the pub trade. His choice was simple. It was almost entirely between the various makes of draught beer, in Sheffield usually bitter. It wasn't fancy; it wasn't exotic or trendy. It was what a man drank and the number of pints sunk at a sitting was considered something to boast about. Men with huge capacities for beer were looked up to and, if this capacity was exceptional, were venerated in their small community. It doesn't happen so much now, but it was what happened then and it was, strangely, by its very existence, comforting.

Today, and it has reached this point only after probably twenty years or so of gradual, almost imperceptible change, this type of customer is at best ignored, at worst actively discouraged. No public house manager wants a bar full of beery middle aged or elderly men drinking pints of bitter and playing dominos all night! He wants, probably because his bosses demand it, the young people. These are the customers, so he has been informed, or perhaps he has observed for himself, who are the big spenders of today. They are the ones who will buy the lager with the strange sounding name or drink by the neck the bottles of strong beer which have been especially brewed for them.

The older customers soon realise the change in what was once their "local". They feel uncomfortable; the things that have changed are not what they want or are happy with. So they slip quietly away and leave the field clear for even more "improvements".

This is not a phenomenon solely restricted to the licenced trade. The pursuit of mammon is widespread. It is called, so I have been informed, progress - I don't like it much. I don't pretend to. But then I was never supposed to like it. I'm a target, not a quarry!

The slaughter of the small, comfortable, local brewery that I was once allowed to cherish is almost complete.

There it is. I've had my whinge, I've written my piece. I know that I'm an old fogy. I should do, for I've been called it so often that I can wear the remark like a baggy old anorak!

I have, during my researches, recorded 52 sites in Sheffield where beer used to be brewed. This is, of course, not counting the pubs which brewed on their own premises. These sites were all within the tight town environs of the 19th century. They weren't all large breweries and many of them would very probably only have supplied a very limited number of pubs, mostly I suspect, the beer-houses which used to be the dominant type of public house in Sheffield, especially in the heavy industrial areas such as Attercliffe.

To try to find a pattern regarding the dates when these breweries both opened and closed, I concentrated on the 32 breweries about which I was fairly certain of both the date on which they opened and the date that they either closed or disappeared into the greedy maw of some larger brewery.

Out of these 32 breweries, I discovered that 19 had opened between the relatively narrow time span of 20 years - between 1840 and 1860. There were two other groups between 1829 and 1833 when five breweries opened and between 1889 and 1892 when four opened. Of the remaining four, two opened in the 18th century and two in the 19th century - one in 1865 and one in 1870.

Why was there such a glut of new companies entering the brewing business in the middle years of the 19th century? I don't know for certain, but it appears reasonable to suppose that it was on the back of the amazingly fast growth in the steel and cutlery industries which Sheffield enjoyed during these years and the corresponding rise in the population. Likewise in the few years earlier, between 1829 and 1833, when the town, as it was then, first began to experience properly organised industries and began to expand and grow. During the years 1831 to 1861, people flooded into the area and the recorded population figures doubled from 92,000 to 185,000.

It is more difficult to explain the closure of the breweries. Some were simply taken over by larger or more prosperous concerns keen on expanding and the original names faded away, often along with the breweries themselves. There is a distinct group of closures between 1898 and 1914, when 15 names either disappeared or changed and another group between 1954 and 1962, which accounted for six companies.

I could, of course, concoct some extremely erudite reason for these closures and no-one would probably argue, but in truth I feel that to find a reason which would sound plausible enough would involve a fairly long investigation into such things as the business climate of the times and, let's face it, the answers wouldn't be very interesting. I think that the reason for the fact is less important than the fact itself. They went - a great many of them! Enough said.

I have chosen three of Sheffield's breweries to research in some depth. There was no particular reason for choosing these three, they just popped into my head. They are, or were, names well known in the city - Tennant Brothers Ltd; SH Wards Ltd and Duncan Gilmour Ltd.

Of these three names, both Tennant's and Gilmour's have disappeared through takeovers. At the time of writing this, Ward's has been closed for about two years having failed to agree to a management takeover with its then overall owner, Swallow Hotels. My understanding of the machinations of big business is limited, so I can't opine much about the future of Ward's pubs. Some company will own them, but whether the Ward's name will survive I don't know.

During my potted history of the following breweries, I have devoted a great deal of space to what may seem to be an inordinate number of take-overs and mergers. Please bear with me on this. I have included this information to illustrate why breweries became fewer and the remaining companies larger until we reach today's situation where a mere handful of multi-national concerns control almost all the brewing activities in the country.

DUNCAN GILMOUR & COMPANY LTD, LADY'S BRIDGE BREWERY, BRIDGE STREET, SHEFFIELD

Before I began to delve into the cobwebbed archives of this company, I must say that I had always thought that it was a smallish wines and spirits dealer, which branched out into brewing. Now I know better. It was in fact a very large company, who were not only wines and spirits dealers, but who also owned large bonded warehouses and who were whisky blenders and exporters. The brewery part of this empire seems to have been almost an afterthought.

I have studied an article written in a publication called, "The Century's Progress". This covers the year 1893 and it furnishes a clear account of Duncan Gilmour's activities since its founding in the mid-19th century. Part of the account was concerned with their bonded warehouses which apparently covered "many acres" and had recently been enlarged. Blending whisky, using their own vats, was carried out not only in Sheffield, but also in Liverpool, Glasgow and Dublin. It can be imagined that when the article states that "they are rewarded by having now a large and ever increasing trade, and a reputation for whisky, not only in the United Kingdom, but on the Continent, in India, China, Egypt, South America and the colonies" this was indeed far more than just a local brewery company.

From The Foundry and Firkin, West St

This is not my present concern, however - my interest is in the local brewery.

This began when Gilmour's added public houses to their business empire and needed to supply them with beer. This prompted the purchase of a site in Furnival Gate which was known as Furnival Brewery. This was in 1860.

When the brewery proved to be a successful venture and had expanded to the extent of outgrowing its premises, the brewery of WH Birks was purchased. This was at Lady's Bridge Brewery, Bridge Street and was bought in 1900. Birks' Brewery was a long established company having first started in business in 1791 when it was known as Nanson & Co. They had used Lady's Bridge Brewery since the middle of the 19th century.

TRADE MARK.

H. J. DEARDEN,
ALE, BEER,
Porter & Bitter Beer
— BREWER, —
HIGH HOUSE BREWERY,
❖ HILLFOOT ❖

There then followed a period of large and fairly rapid expansion for Gilmour's. In 1901, the company took over **H J Dearden's Brewery**, which was established c1833 and which owned **High House Brewery**, Bamforth Street, off Penistone Road. This company didn't own any public houses themselves, but relied on supplying beer to the free-houses of the area. This was Gilmour's objective. This old and long abandoned brewery - Gilmour's never used it for brewing, existed until late 1999-early 2000 in an almost complete state and could be seen from Penistone Road, especially the chimney.

The buildings were used by various small business ventures like a fencing manufacturer and a car spares firm. Now, with the chimney reduced to almost nothing and much of the remaining brewery demolished, the site is in the process of being "modernised" and built over.

The next acquisition was the brewery of Whitmarsh & Watson, Free Trade Brewery, South Street, The Moor. This company had come about as the result of an amalgamation between the breweries of William Whitmarsh & Co, Earl Street - who had taken over William Jepson's Brewery in 1854 - and John Watson's Spring Lane Brewery in 1898. Whitmarsh & Watson took over Wilson Brothers Parkside Brewery, Sussex Street in 1900 before being themselves absorbed by Gilmour's empire in 1906. This merger added some 140 public houses to the Duncan Gilmour stable. Complicated, isn't it?

Two more additions were to follow. In 1910, **William Greaves Norfolk Brewery**, Broad Street, Park was taken over and this was followed, after a lull of many years in 1946, by what remained of Sheffield's oldest commercial brewery, Thomas Rawson & Co. Ltd, Pond Street.

This brewery had been damaged by German bombing during December, 1940. The object of the takeover, as is usual in the brewing trade, seems to have been gaining control of the tied houses still under the Rawson banner. Thus disappeared the name of **Thomas Rawson's Brewery**, which had been producing beer on the Pond Street site since c1758.

Having gobbled up their fair share of small fish, Gilmour's were, in 1954, taken over by Joshua Tetley's Brewery of Leeds. At this time, Gilmour's either owned or controlled about 342 public houses, some of which were probably still beer-houses, and had built up a large free-trade thanks to its own shrewd business exploits.

The Hallamshire Hotel, West St

It came as no surprise when Tetley's closed Lady's Bridge Brewery, but kept the pubs! This grand old brewery was later demolished, along with its brewery tap, The Bridge Inn, to facilitate extensions to the magistrates court and police

Rawson's Brewery, Pond Street

headquarters. The Bridge Inn was commonly called The Little Bridge and was popular with the local Irish. Only strong men drank there!

Tetley's themselves were soon afterwards to become a part of the giant Allied Breweries combine. And so it rolls on...

Although the name of Duncan Gilmour has disappeared from the brewing industry, there are still several public houses in Sheffield which sport the legend, Duncan Gilmour's Windsor Ales, across the front. The Rutland Arms, Brown Street is one and another attractive, old pub which does so is **The Dog & Partridge, Trippet Lane**. This extinct name can also be seen etched into the window glass of pubs in Sheffield, as is still to be seen at the Foundry and Firkin.

Why Windsor Ales? From 1902 until 1915, Gilmour's controlled - I'm not sure if they ever actually owned it - **The Windsor Brewery**, Upper Parliament Street, Liverpool. This company's logo was Windsor Castle and I can only suppose that Gilmour's liked it and added it to their business advertising. Perhaps it seemed like a good idea at the time and it stuck. I am sure that Gilmour's had nothing to do with Windsor in Berkshire.

Referring again to the article in "The Century's Progress", I should like to quote an interesting piece about Gilmour's:-

"During recent years, Messrs Duncan Gilmour & Co Ltd, have added considerably to their renown by solving that difficult problem, the production of a satisfactory non-intoxicating substitute for beer. This they have accomplished in their now famous Hop Bitter Beer, which is brewed at Sheffield and Liverpool, and also supplied in cask to between two and three thousand bottlers throughout Great Britain and Ireland. They have also arranged to export it, and have already made several large shipments to the United States and Canada."

The following is a quotation, included in the above magazine, from The Whisky Trade Review. This august publication says:-

"The lion may truly lie down with the lamb. The moderate drinker and the teetotaller may now enter a refreshment bar together, call for Gilmour's Hops, toast the Queen, the President, the King etc., repeat the order, toast themselves, and go on their way, no-one's susceptibilities having been harmed in the least." Well, I never!

I wonder is anyone else has ever heard of this stuff? I certainly hadn't and don't feel any the worse for that. Actually, although the magazine article gives the impression that this muck was brewed exclusively by Gilmour's, I have searched around and found that other breweries produced the same sort of rubbish. It was reputed to have been very popular with agricultural workers. I come from East Anglia, and the farm workers that I knew as a boy seemed to exist on either cold tea or warm beer!

SH WARD & Co Ltd, SHEAF BREWERY, ECCLESALL ROAD

The story of this brewery really begins with a Lincolnshire corn merchants, a man named George and an unpaid bill.

I have studied various documents and I have found dates quoted when things happened at and to this brewery and I'm not convinced that all of them make sense. For example, in a quarterly newsletter, published by Ward's Brewery and entitled Innsight, dated Winter, 1972, it states that the story of the brewery starts in the 1830's when George Wright first came to Sheffield. As George Wright died in 1910 aged 78, then he must have been born in c1832 and was thus quite obviously too young in the

From the Riverside Tavern, formerly the Brown Cow, Nursery Street.

1830's to have been travelling anywhere. This statement then is a mistake and as I don't propose to copy other peoples' mistakes, God knows, I make enough of my own, I am going to write an account of this brewery based on what facts I know are true.

Sometime in the middle of the 19th century, George Wright was dispatched from Lincolnshire by his corn merchant father-in-law to Sheffield to see a Mr John Kirby of Sheaf Island Brewery, Effingham Road. The reason for the journey was to discuss the non-payment of a large bill for a load of malted barley that the brewery had received. It was a journey which was to change George Wright's life and was the first step towards the setting up of a family dynasty in Sheffield's brewing industry.

Mr Kirby was in financial trouble; the brewery wasn't paying its way and it seemed that bankruptcy was looming - not an uncommon state of affairs in brewing. However, another way out of his trouble was found. One that was more intelligent and which would satisfy both parties and keep the business going.

The corn merchants, realising that the only hope of getting their money was to get the brewery back on its financial feet, persuaded Mr Kirby to allow George Wright, whose business sense was well thought of by his employers, to take charge of the financial side of the brewery and see what he could do, with survival in mind.

The agreement was a success. George applied his business brain to the task and the brewery began to prosper. This could well have been the end of the story with George going back to Lincolnshire, but it wasn't. George realised that not only did he like working at the brewery, but he also liked living in Sheffield. He decided to make a radical change in his life, one that was going to affect his descendants right down as far as his great-grandson. He moved his wife and family, lock, stock and barrel, to Sheffield and set up a partnership with John Kirby which resulted in the creation of the forerunner to SH Wards & Co Ltd, Kirby, Wright & Co.

Things went along pretty well at first for the new brewery and by the 1860's the future looked promising, until a mistake by George Wright once again plunged the company into deep and murky financial waters.

Using his share of the brewery partnership as a surety, he stood as guarantor for a relative who had invested heavily in the cargo of one of the tea clippers which in those days plied regularly between India and England. The ship was lost, as often happened, as was its cargo, and the bank, which had loaned the money for the venture, began to make threatening noises - as banks are apt to do. The brewery seemed once again to be heading for the sharp financial rocks of the bankruptcy court.

It was saved by the timely intervention of a local businessman, Septimus Henry Ward. Mr Ward must have seen potential in the business and he injected sufficient capital which not only saved the brewery, but also allowed enough money to spare to finance further expansion. And expand it did!

Still known in the 1880's as Kirby, Wright & Co, the company acquired two local breweries, both situated in Ecclesall Road - **The Albion Brewery** and Bradley's Soho Brewery.

The Albion Brewery had begun its life in c1840 and had a succession of names and owners. It was first Hunt's Albion Brewery. This changed in 1859 to Hunt, Fernell & Warhurst Ltd and later, in 1871, to Hunt & Co. In the late 1870's, it changed again to **Peter Lowe & Co**, but this was short-lived as by 1883, it was called DH Coupe & Co. The brewery was then briefly owned by **Latham & Quihampton** who sold it to Kirby, Wright & Co.

For a short time both the Sheaf Island Brewery and the Albion Brewery were

used by Kirby, Wright, but after the purchase of Bradley's Soho Brewery, which was followed soon afterwards by its modernisation and improvement with all the latest brewing equipment, the Albion Brewery was sold to a rival and became known as the **Old Albion Brewing Company**. This company was taken over in 1939 by the Worksop & Retford Brewing Company and closed down. The site was sold to the tool-makers, James Neill and Co Ltd.

There is an interesting piece of history attached to Bradley's Soho Brewery. When it was first conceived, the two partners were Mr William Bradley of Manor Oaks and Mr John Newton Mappin of Clarkehouse Street. Mr Bradley has sunk, historically, without trace, but JN Mappin was of a different calibre.

He was born in 1800, the son of Joseph Mappin, a successful engraver with his own business. He went to Milk Street School, Sharrow Vale and

PETER LOWE & COMP.

Mild & Bitter Beer,

STOUT & PORTER

BREWERS,

ALBION BREWERY,

ECCLESALL ROAD,

SHEFFIELD.

then began work at his father's firm as a silver engraver and designer. He must, at some time, have become a partner in the firm, for he was able to sell his share to his nephew, JY Cowlishaw and in the late 1830's he embarked on what was to be a fairly short partnership with Mr Bradley. After this was dissolved, he bought the Masbrough Old Brewery, Greasbrough Road, Rotherham. It was this purchase and his business acumen which made him the wealthy man that he became. Probably the most obvious outward indication of his success was the purchase of his large house, named Birchlands, in Ranmoor, sometime in the 1850's.

Some wealthy men leave behind a statue or an ornate tomb, but JN Mappin went much better than that and left a legacy to the city of his birth, which has kept his name alive while memories of far wealthier and more influential men have faded away. It has also given pleasure to many thousands of people - The Mappin Art Gallery, Weston Park.

It seems obvious from a study of his later life that, as soon as he could afford it, he became an avid, perhaps even an obsessive collector of paintings. It is said that during one period of 15 years, he spent about £60,000 on art. That must be the modern day equivalent of about £2 million.

I don't want to delve too deeply into his life, or the lives of his nephews, Sir Frederick Thorpe Mappin and JY Cowlishaw. After all, this is a book about pubs. But if you would like more information about this Sheffield businessman and benefactor, then I can recommend "In Perpetuity and Without Charge". This book was published by the Mappin Art Gallery to commemorate its 100th anniversary.

To continue - now with a large and modern brewery on the Soho Brewery site, the original Sheaf Island Brewery in Effingham Road was closed and sold to the Sheffield Gas Company. The Soho Brewery was then renamed the Sheaf Brewery - the name it retained until the brewery closed recently.

The name of Kirby, Wright & Co disappeared when, in 1896, it was registered as SH Ward & Co Ltd.

Another brewery was added to Ward's strength in February, 1890, when it bought Lofthouse & Bell of Eldon Street. This small concern was first known as Carter & Smith in c1854. It then became Joseph Smith's Eldon Brewery; then Smith & Lofthouse and finally Lofthouse & Bell. A lot of names for a small brewery!

In the early days of Kirby, Wright and later SH Ward, the company faced the same problem which all local brewers had to solve - brewing your beer was the easy part, the difficult part was to sell it! This, in those days, wasn't an easy task and had to be worked at if the company was to thrive, or even to survive.

Most of the public houses in the 19th century, be they full public houses or merely ale- or beer-houses, were what would today be termed "free" houses. That is they were privately owned and not "tied" to a brewery. This meant that they could shop around for the brewery that would give them the best deal on the price of beer. I've no doubt that there was a great deal of playing one brewery off against another. That's what I would have done! It was, and still is, a cut-throat business. Indeed, it wasn't unusual for a pub to buy beer from no-one and to brew its own.

Later, of course, Ward's did what all breweries did, and still do, they built up their own chain of public houses and thus had a captive customer for their beers. This is why breweries are always keen to swallow up the competition. Ward's kept the pubs that it gained from its take-overs and they bought any other pubs that they could. It was, at one time, a company policy to only own or supply one pub in any village and this perhaps accounts for the wide spread of Ward's pubs.

In the 1870's, the brewery employed three sales representatives, one a lady, to go out and sell their beer. The one who covered the outlying country areas used a pony and trap for transport. It was said that of the two, often only the pony knew the way home!

These were the days of horsepower and all the breweries used a large number of dray horses to transport their beer around the town. The out of town deliveries usually went at least part of the way by train and then by local carrier. Things were slower then.

Of course, as the 20th century progressed, motor vehicles of one sort or another took over from the horses, but it wasn't until 1931 that the Ward's dray horses disappeared completely from the streets. Even then a small stable was maintained for a few horses which were kept for display purposes as some breweries still do today. Actually, the date 1931, seems to me to be rather early for the total demise of Ward's dray horses. I can remember seeing horses on the streets of Nottingham in the early 1950's, These were used by Shipstone's Brewery. But then Nottingham has always lagged rather behind Sheffield, hasn't it?

The two main founders of the brewery both died in the early years of the 20th century - SH Ward in 1906 and George Wright in 1910, aged 78 years old. Already the next generation had grasped the reins of power. Charles Ward, William Wright and his brother, Richard, had been directors since the end of the 19th century.

The name of Kirby doesn't seem to have carried on in the company through into the 20th century; the Ward name only seems to have carried on for one generation, but the family of George Wright were to control the brewery right up to its end.

In the late 1960's, Wilfrid Wright, the grandson of George and company chairman, realised that his brewery was likely to soon become a target for take-over interest and would, inevitably sooner or later, fall victim to a larger company. He took the sensible business decision to choose which company Ward's would merge with. In effect, he decided to jump, before he was pushed. So, in 1972, SH Ward's joined forces with the Vaux Brewery of Sunderland.

It worked very well and one of the first policy decisions made after this merger was that Ward's Brewery would continue under its own name and, to all intents and purposes, still produce its own branded beers and operate as a local brewery.

Unfortunately, when both Ward's and Vaux were taken over by a larger group, the decision was made to either sell them as going concerns or to close them. Although I feel that the option to close them was the one most favoured by the new parent company.

It seems that these days it is cheaper and more profitable for a company that owns pubs to "outsource" the beer that it requires. I like to use modern jargon when I can! I neither know, nor care what happened to Vaux, but I do know that following a failed attempt at a management buyout, the Sheaf Brewery of SH Ward Ltd. closed in July, 1999. What will happen to the derelict site is, at the time of writing, unknown.

During the 1970's and 1980's, when the future looked cloudless, most of the original brewery was demolished in order that new and more modern bottling, brewing and office facilities could be built. This means that a large part of the brewery is historically uninteresting and not really worth keeping. Only the original gates and the tower which date back I believe to the first Soho Brewery, are historic gems. Perhaps, in years to come, when the site has been "developed", these features will be absorbed into some architectural plans. Who knows? I'm afraid that one more local brewery has fallen in the cause of progress.

Although Ward's was never the largest brewery in Sheffield, it stayed the course for many years, prospered and outlived a number of larger breweries. When it closed it was, in fact, the last large commercial brewery left in Sheffield.

From a purely personal point of view, I never particularly liked Ward's beers. Perhaps, as a Southerner, I wasn't ready for them. I did like their pubs, though. They were among the best in the city.

TENNANT BROTHERS LTD, EXCHANGE BREWERY, BRIDGE STREET

There can't be many breweries in England that were built on at least part of the site of a castle. This one was.

When the Tennant brothers, Edward and Robert, first entered into the brewing business, they took over the Exchange Brewery of Proctor & Co. As this was situated almost opposite the old corn exchange, the brewery name was derived from that.

The Exchange Brewery 2000

Proctor's had been in business since c1820 and it was in 1840 that the Tennants' became the owners. It was about this time in Sheffield's history that a large number of breweries first started up.

I've no idea what depth of knowledge the brothers had about the brewing business. It might well have been rather sketchy and it was probably a relief when they managed to get a competent businessman to join them. This was in 1847.

Thomas Moore was not born in Sheffield. He came from Howden, East Yorkshire and was 38 years old and already a wealthy man when he moved to the town. It seems that he became interested in the Exchange Brewery, because he wanted to be involved in a local company where he could use both his business skills and money to the best advantage. He turned out to be just what the brewery needed and it wasn't long before he was proving his worth.

In either 1851 or 1852, while the company was moving along smoothly and the future was looking good, the brewery's landlord, the Duke of Norfolk, through his land agent, dropped a large spanner into the business works. He wanted to develop the site upon which the brewery stood and put up a covered market hall. This meant that the brewery and everything else which stood on the site, between Dixon Lane, The

The Exchange Brewery 1999

Haymarket, Exchange Street and Castle Folds, would be demolished. This included The Tontine Hotel, which was one of the largest and oldest coaching inns in the town.

The duke instructed his agent to refuse to renew the brewery's lease when it ran out, as was soon to be the case. In effect, he wanted to evict the brewery. It was a very high-handed decision, especially as no compensation was to be paid for the new buildings and other improvements that Tennant Bros. had made to the site. Thomas Moore was mightily upset and rightly so.

He made it clear to the duke's agent that if they were forced to move, then they wanted additional time added to the current lease to allow for the time needed in either setting up or buying a new brewery together with compensation for the cost of all the upheaval and for the site improvements.

Things, as they sometimes do in business, got very nasty and of course the lawyers appeared out of the woodwork. There were proposals, counter-proposals and threats until finally the matter came up for judgement before the Lord Chief Justice of England, Lord Campbell, at York Chancery Court.

After much long and no doubt expensive legal argument, a compromise was reached in the best English tradition. This more or less satisfied both sides, probably because no-one thought that they'd get a better deal. It was agreed that Tennant Bros. would vacate the site, but would be allowed a four month period of grace to use in finding a new site. They would also be compensated in the sum of £3,000 for their trouble. The duke got his land back.

Four months isn't long in which to set up a new brewery and Thomas Moore wasted none of it - he had probably been working on things while the court case dragged on - and he found a site within a few hundred yards of the original brewery. It was on the banks of the River Don a little way downstream from where the first Lady's Bridge was built.

The new buildings were erected, the brewery moved and brewing recommenced, all within the four month deadline. According to reports of the time "not a brewing was lost!"

This new brewery, which retained the Exchange Brewery name, was built on what had once been the site of at least part of Sheffield castle. This fortification had been a thorn in the side of the Parliamentary Army during the Civil War and in 1648, following an Act of Parliament, it was demolished. At the time the new brewery was built, the River Don supported many water wheels used for grinding and drop stamping and in fact one was taken over by Tennant Bros. to use as a bottle store. The muddy track which ran past the brewery was to become Bridge Street very soon after the brewery was built.

It is worth doing a sketch of Thomas Moore's life. He was an interesting man. He was, during the many years that he lived in Sheffield until his death in 1880, among the most valuable men in the town. He was a businessman of great vision, who had not only the capital resources, but also the courage to push through any project he felt was worthwhile. This applied both to his personal life and to his services to the town.

He became a town councillor in 1862, an office which he served with great diligence. He was proposed by Thomas Jessop, the industrialist and former mayor himself in 1863/4, for the office of mayor and he was unique in serving the town in this capacity for four years, from 1868 to 1871. He was made an Alderman of Sheffield in 1873.

His death at the age of 70 must have come as a major blow to Tennant Bros, but the business carried on and in 1882, it was registered as a limited company.

The founders and original directors, Edward and Robert Tennant, don't seem to figure much in the history of the brewery, apart from giving it a name. It is perhaps a fair assumption, and it is only that, they left most of the business decisions to Thomas Moore and then they either retired, died, or just left the business. I can find neither of their names in any trade directory of the period. Nor do they seem to have involved themselves in the local politics of the town to any noticeable extent.

Following the decision to become a limited company, Tennant's began to expand with some vigour and by the turn of the century, they owned around 100 public houses of all types - the lifeblood of a successful brewery. These hadn't been acquired by the usual means of taking over rival breweries, but had almost all been bought as privately owned "free" houses. These were the pubs which formed the backbone of the trade in the 19th century. In the first three-quarters of this century they almost died out, but now as the business climate changes, they are returning.

The first buy was a vintners, Wiley & Company. This gave Tennant's a strong say in the wines and spirits trade in Sheffield and its surrounding area.

Then came the breweries. **In 1916, AH Smith's Don Brewery**, Penistone Road; in 1918, **Strout's Burton Road Brewery;** in 1924, Thomas Berry & Co, Ecclesall Brewery, Moorhead. All these breweries were stripped of their assets, which mostly meant their pubs, and then either closed as brewing concerns and used for storage, or closed completely. The object of buying them had been merely to strengthen Tennant's stable of public houses.

More acquisitions were to follow and indeed were still being absorbed into the parent company right up to the time that Tennant's themselves were swallowed up.

In 1944, the Nottingham Brewery Company was taken over. This was a substantial asset gained as the Nottingham business had its own subsidiaries, which included the

ESTABLISHED 1832.

Telegraphic Address:
"DON BREWERY, SHEFFIELD."

Telephone No. 319.

A. H. SMITH & CO. LTD.,
DON BREWERY,
PENISTONE ROAD,
SHEFFIELD,
BREWERS OF
MILD AND STRONG ALES,
BITTER BEER AND STOUT,
LIGHT BITTER BEER FOR FAMILY USE
At 1/- per gallon, in 9, 12 and 18 gall. Casks.

BOTTLERS OF ALE AND STOUT.

WINE, SPIRIT AND CIGAR
MERCHANTS.
SOLE PROPRIETORS OF THE FAMOUS
"GLEN SHEE" SPECIAL SCOTCH WHISKY,
AND THE
"SHAN" SPECIAL IRISH WHISKY.

Wellow Brewery in Grimsby; the Cardington Brewery Company in Bedfordshire and James Rose & Co of Nettleton, Lincolnshire.

In a rather unusual joint business deal with William Stones Ltd, Tennant's in 1954 gained part ownership of the Sheffield Free Brewery, Queen's Brewery, Queen's Road. This brewery had once been known as Rhoden, Freeman & Co, but it had failed and been reborn as the Sheffield Free Brewery. A year after this deal, Tennant's assumed full ownership of the brewery.

A stronghold was gained in Barnsley in 1958 following the take-over of Clarkson's Old Brewery, Wood Street, Barnsley.

This company owned about 60 public houses and although the brewery buildings were soon demolished, the Clarkson's trademark, an elephant, could and perhaps can still be seen, etched into the window glass of some of their former pubs.

I believe that another Barnsley area purchase was Lang's Brewery, but of this I can find out nothing.

The final, largest and most important buy made by Tennant's was the Worksop & Retford Brewery, Priorwell Brewery, Worksop. This brewery had, in 1939, absorbed the Old Albion Brewery, Ecclesall Road, which had once been owned by SH Ward & Co.

This final plunge into the take-over pool netted Tennant's 192 public

STROUTS AND WATERMAN,

BREWERS,

BURTON ROAD BREWERY,

SHEFFIELD.

houses and brought the number of pubs owned by the company to about 700. This, of course, was quite apart from the various other companies they owned in the soft drinks and other related trades. It was a big brewery. It was a tempting target!

When, in 1962, Tennant Brothers Ltd, became part of Whitbread (East Pennines) Ltd, it was one of Whitbread's largest subsidiaries.

It was a great loss both to the local brewing industry in Yorkshire and to the City of

Sheffield, when the Exchange Brewery was shut down in July, 1993. Although a large part of the brewery complex, which has since been demolished, could perhaps be described at best as industrially picturesque and at worse downright ugly, its passing has removed a certain vibrancy from that end of the city, both in bustle and smell. The Grade II listed office and brewery tap section which remain was at first rather attractive, then it became dowdy as time and weather both made their marks and now it is beginning to look little short of derelict. Which, of course, is what it is. Although this month, August 2000, the developers of the brewery site - the Totty construction company plc and others have covered the building in scaffolding and conversion work is afoot.

As with many closed down, but still remembered breweries, the new owners, mostly for financial reasons I suspect, often try to keep the old brand names going, but they never seem quite the same, do they? Except in the case of Tennant's **Gold Label Barley Wine**. This is still on the market and, as far as I'm concerned, it will always be a good drink.

A postscript to this account, which has a connection to Tennant's Brewery, is that Thomas Kingsford Wilson was, during some early part of this century, chairman of the brewery. He was a great grandson of Joseph Wilson (1723 - 1796), who is generally regarded as the founder of the snuff makers, Wilson & Co (Sharrow) Ltd.

He lived at Fulwood House and was dedicated to game shooting. This sporting obsession was helped by the fact that the Wilson family owned moors at Moscar, Stanage and Bamford - about 6,500 acres of them. He also had friends with similar land holdings.

According to an appendix included in "The Wilsons of Sharrow" by Mark Chaytor, himself a member of the Wilson family, during an active game shooting career of 50 seasons, from 1885 to 1934, Mr Wilson killed 149,978 animals! This was, of course, at no small cost to himself. The average animal cost him 2.09 cartridges - a total of 313,810 cartridges over the duration of his "career"!

It amazes me that lists were kept which actually recorded things like this in such fine detail that a decimal point per cartridge was noted.

Who says that rich men fritter their lives away?

last orders

CHAPTER TWO
NEW PUBS FROM OLD BUILDINGS

As the commercial face of Sheffield changed during the last ten years or so and the attitude relaxed of the previously over zealous licencing magistrates - those little tin gods who, unasked, took it upon themselves to overseer our moral welfare - opportunities were noticed and seized upon to convert some of the many redundant buildings, mostly in the city centre, to licenced premises.

When I first planned this chapter, I had intended to cover every new/old premises in the city centre and also those in the suburbs. Since then I have taken time to wander round the area and I have realised just how many of these places have quite recently opened up and are still appearing. Most of them are in former shop premises, others are in better known buildings.

I recently took a stroll from The Yorick public house in Division Street, walked to the junction with Cambridge Street and followed the street down to where it joins the Moor. This is only a matter of a couple of hundred yards or so and yet in this short distance there are 13 places licenced to sell alcohol. Out of these, half a dozen are recent additions to the city and only the two regular pubs, The Yorick and The Sportsman, are of any age at all.

This isn't a process that is going to suddenly stop, at least not for a few years and so I have had to revamp this chapter. If I don't, then in the short time before this book is published, so many other places may have opened up that this chapter will seem to be rather dated.

All I am now going to include are a dozen or so of the larger or older premises, the ones that have taken over the buildings which were, at one time, important or well known in the city. That way, I can concentrate my little pearls of knowledge instead of scattering them too widely and sometimes missing the target.

This increase in the number of licenced premises, which are after all only taking over from the many dozens of pubs which have closed in Sheffield this century, I view with pleasure. Saving old and empty buildings from demolition and turning them into something useful and attractive seems to me to be an obvious and welcome course to take. Although, of course, there have been the usual mutterings from some fairly unrepresentative sections of the population, who would have apparently preferred to have seen these buildings knocked down, rather than used for pleasure.

For many years the policy of Sheffield City Council appeared to have been just that - if a building, regardless of its history or architectural merit, was either empty, in the way of yet another hare-brained development scheme or needed a bit of money spending on it, it was razed to the ground. It disappeared for ever. Many fine and irreplaceable buildings have been lost to the city due to this short-sighted attitude. If the City Council had prevailed in the early 1980's and that beautiful slice of theatrical history, The Lyceum Theatre, had been reduced to a heap of rubble, I wonder what would have appeared in its place? Certainly not a pub - more likely a multi-storey carpark! Thankfully and almost too late, this attitude seems to be changing.

I have made a list of the buildings that I intend to include in this chapter and it is surprising the former uses that some of these buildings enjoyed. On a purely personal note, I regularly frequented the building that is now called "The All Bar One", Leopold Street. That was in the days when I had money, before I became a writer and it was a branch of the Abbey National. Now that it is styled a wine bar/cafe bar, it seems bigger and the queues are shorter.

It is a rare pub these days which doesn't offer a good range of food. All the places in this chapter go a little further than that and can rival most restaurant in the variety of dishes on their menus. Most of it seems to be good value and although I obviously haven't tried everything available, the food I have eaten was excellent.

As these buildings are all historically, as pubs, very new, I thought that the best thing that I could do to find out about them was to pay each of them a visit. I know - it's a lousy job, but research must be done!

The Old Library, Ecclesall Road South

As the name suggests, this building was once a public library but, before that happened, it had a variety of uses and owners. It is now owned by Tom Cobleigh Ltd.

It was originally Ecclesall College, but when this closed in 1880, the building was bought by a Mr Crossley who altered it into a private dwelling and called it The Knowle. He sold it in 1892 to Mr John Kingsford Wilson, a steel manufacturer and member of the snuff making family. He renamed it Kingscote.

The next inhabitant, who purchased the building in 1907, was Sir William Ellis. He renamed it Weetwood and following his death in 1945, it was bought by the then Sheffield Corporation who opened it as Ecclesall branch library soon afterwards. There things rested until 1995 when, as a result of one of Sheffield Council's more breathtakingly stupid decisions and in the face of much fierce local opposition, it was closed down as the local library and sold (some more of the "family silver"?).

In 1998 it reopened as a public house and restaurant, The Weetwood House, and then shortly afterwards the name changed to a new and not very sensitive name, The Old Library. It must be like salt in the wounds of the many people who opposed its closure as a library, the only one in the district, every time they see that name. At least it is still the meeting place of the Ecclesall Local History Society.

The All Bar One, Leopold Street

This cafe/bar owes its strange, acutely angled shape to its position on the corner of Leopold Street and Orchard Street. In a previous life it was a branch of the Abbey National and when they moved, it was converted into another money making enterprise. The arms of the Abbey National can still be seen engraved into one of the outside walls - picked out in gold!

Inside, the decor is bland and uninspiring with the customary collection of grainy black and white enlargements of photographs of old Sheffield. It leans more towards serving food rather than drink and although slightly pricey, the service is good and the wine is well above average. It seems to be busiest at lunchtimes probably due to its position near to many offices and also because it isn't all that large.

The Bar Coast, Division Street

This building was once the Divisional Headquarters of the South Yorkshire County Fire Service and from here were controlled 27 fire stations around the region. It was designed in the 1920's by the city architect, W.G Davies and the foundation stone was laid by the then Lord Mayor of Sheffield, Alderman Moses Humberstone. Although square and functional in its design, it does have an attractive facade with various relief sculptures at roof level.

Today, it is a cafe/bar which wears two distinct hats - in the daytime it is the usual place to go for a decent meal, but at night the DJ's rule and it is not the place to take grandad.

The decor is very modern and the inside is spacious with the original glass panelled doors forming a wall with a view into Division Street - if there's anything to look at.

Lloyds No. I, Division Street

This Grade II Listed Building has plenty of history and is a mere 30 yards nearer the city centre than the Bar Coast.

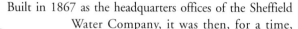

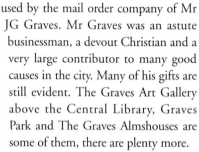

Built in 1867 as the headquarters offices of the Sheffield Water Company, it was then, for a time, used by the mail order company of Mr JG Graves. Mr Graves was an astute businessman, a devout Christian and a very large contributor to many good causes in the city. Many of his gifts are still evident. The Graves Art Gallery above the Central Library, Graves Park and The Graves Almshouses are some of them, there are plenty more.

After standing empty for several years in the 1970's, it was taken over and extended by the National Union of Mineworkers and was intended to be used as the National Headquarters. However, following the rather punitive miners strike of 1984/85, the union split and the membership of the NUM was divided between themselves and the Union of Democratic Mineworkers. The idea of a central headquarters for one union fell by the wayside, there were financial problems because of the cost of building the large, modern extension at the rear of the complex and, before it became Lloyd's No. I, it was fast becoming a white elephant of a building.

Today it is a split level, large and airy establishment which is rather staid and quiet during the day and on most evenings, but earns its corn for the owners during the weekend.

RSVP, Cambridge Street

This is almost opposite Lloyd's No. 1 and shouldn't really be in this chapter - it is not a new pub in an old building. Rather, it is brand new having opened for business on Friday 13th August, 1999. Obviously the owners, Whitbread NE Ltd, are not superstitious! But as it is rather unique by being a large building actually built as a pub and as there aren't enough of those to make a chapter, I slipped it in here. It is built, together with a couple of shop units and, I believe, some flats, on the corner site which was, for many years, occupied by **The Albert**. This was a

The Albert

34

seriously old pub which had first opened for business, probably as a beer-house before 1797. It was closed and demolished, much to the disgust of its regulars, in 1988 because of severe structural damage caused by mining subsidence.

If this sounds weird in the centre of a city, it was because many years ago there used to be a small, drift mine which produced coal during the 18th century at the bottom of Cambridge Street, which was at that time called Coal Pit Lane. The site of the mine is somewhere beneath where the Moor shopping area is today. In those far back days, this was where Sheffield ended and from there on it was nothing much until you got to Ecclesall, but rough pasture and moorland. At one time, there used to be a racecourse in the area.

It was said that anyone of substance who wished to travel to Ecclesall and beyond during the hours of darkness was well advised to hire the services, as an escort, of a couple of large men with stout cudgels to protect them from the footpads and other assorted villains who roamed the area. Happy days!

The Albert changed its name from The Union in honour of the consort of Queen Victoria, Prince Albert of Saxe-Coburg-Gotha. I wonder if this stiff necked and rather intense man was pleased? I wonder, in fact, if he had ever even heard of Sheffield. There used to be at least four other "Albert" pubs in the city, but only the one in Darnall Road remains. Cambridge Street was also named after royalty. Probably after the Duke of Cambridge, 1774-1850. He was the youngest of the seven sons of George III.

When I paid a visit to the **RSVP** a fortnight after it had opened, I found a rather large and barn like premises, sparsely furnished and obviously built to cater for the circuit of young drinkers who revolve round the centre of Sheffield during the weekend.

I hope that the contractors who built the corner complex made sure that there wouldn't be a repeat of the subsidence that finished off the old Albert pub. I shall wait and see. It may take a few years to show - it did before!

By the way. Before I left RSVP, as a joke, I asked the bar manager what the initials stood for. She hadn't a clue. So much for modern education.

The Bankers Draft, Market Place

The Market Place used to be where, in the previous centuries, the market stalls were set up and farmers brought beasts and produce to sell. It hasn't been used for that purpose for many years and, before it became what it now is, a stopping place for the Supertram, it was mainly used as a subterranean system of pedestrian underpasses known, with typical Sheffield bluntness, as "the hole in the road". This was all filled in at huge expense when the Supertram became a reality in 1993.

The Grade II Listed Building which is now the Banker's Draft was formerly a branch of the Midland Bank, now known as the HSBC. This stands for, I believe, The Hong Kong & Shanghai Banking Corporation - whatever next? It is part of the JD Wetherspoon group - the pub, not the bank!

Again, as with most of the "new from old" watering holes in the city centre, this is quite pleasant and suitable for any age of customer during the day, but aims for the young, upmarket big spenders in the evenings. It is on a split level giving two floors, it has a no smoking area and claims to hold about 1,500 people, but seats less than that. No jeans or football colours here, please - it says so on the door.

The Ferret and Trouserleg, St. James Street

I gave this pub a brief mention in the first volume of this book. That was before it adopted its silly name. Not much else has changed, though, except that it has begun to show its age and is becoming, compared to some of the newer places, just that wee bit tatty at the corners.

This seems, from the outside, to be a larger building than it is and was at one time owned by the Church of England. It was either a dormitory for minor members of the clergy or a choir school or possibly both. It was abandoned for many years and for a period in the 1980's it was the home of a variety of squatters. I am rather surprised that it isn't a listed buiding.

When the Church sold it to The Wolverhampton & Dudley Brewery, the new owners, naturally enough, wanted to turn it into a public house of some sort. The Church objected, but to be frank, what did they expect a brewery to do with a newly bought building? Turn it into a flower shop?

There then resulted a fairly bitter and prolonged planning battle between the two sides. Common sense, however, prevailed and the brewery converted the building into more of a pub than a cafe bar. It has a nice collection of Spy cartoons on the walls, along with a large array of TV screens. Again the elders rule during daylight hours and the young bloods appear at night. I wonder when it will get rid of the name?

The Sheaf Quays, Wharf Street

This was at one time the largest and most complete factory complex in Sheffield. It was built at a cost of some £50,000 in the 1820's by William Greaves & Sons. After passing through several hands, it eventually fell derelict and today only the main office building is left. Until it was taken in hand and refurbished it was in a very dilapidated condition.

Now, it is owned by Tom Cobleigh Ltd and is a complicated mixture of cafe/bar, public house, restaurant and night spot. It also has a function suite and for those of you who are fenestration freaks, it has 70 windows. I am again rather surprised that it isn't a listed building, but it doesn't appear to be so.

The area that it is part of, The Canal Basin, has been beautifully restored and in the summer it is difficult to believe that the centre of Sheffield is only a matter of yards away. It seems a shame that, apart from the a few canal boats, it is little used or visited.

The Old Monk, Norfolk Street

Another Grade II Listed Building which used to be a Trustee Savings Bank until a couple of years ago. Then it was remodelled and became The Fraternity House. However, due I believe to a change of ownership, it soon became The Old Monk.
When I first had a look in the place it was midday and I got the impression of a huge, echoing, bus-station like place. This is inevitable, I suppose, if you want plenty of room for the night-time customers. As is to be expected it carries a detailed menu and a good range of drinks. Not my sort of place, but then it wasn't made with the likes of me in mind.

Aunt Sally's, Clarkehouse Road

This was formerly a residential building, but has been extended and modernised within the constrictions of its Grade II Listed Building status. It is now a reasonable public house cum eating house. Owned by Tom Cobleigh Ltd, it had, when privately owned, a large and pleasantly maintained garden. It now has a large carpark! I expect with the close proximity of the seats of learning, known, I believe, as Sheffield University, it will never be short of youthful patronage.

Hanrahan's Bar, Glossop Road

Very near to Aunt Sally's, this can expect the same sort of customer. It is a Grade II Listed Building (another?) and was once owned by Sheffield University. There was a planning wrangle, which I know little about, when it was planned to demolish what was then an attractive short terrace of what might be Georgian houses. Now, they have been converted into this upmarket licenced premises with an Irish name. They have recently survived another refurbishment. So soon after the original conversion it makes me wonder if they are looking for the right "theme" to attract customers.

The Player's Cafe, Arena Leisure Park, Attercliffe Road

The building which houses this extravagant mixture of most types of licenced premises was built in 1874 to provide a primary school for the Attercliffe area. During the 91 years of its school life, It provided education for many thousands of the children of the miners, steel workers and cutlery workers who crowded into the long rows of terraced houses which existed beneath the shadows of the huge steelworks.

When it closed in 1965, the city council, with a typical lack of foresight, allowed it to rot and become the target for any thief or vandal who cared to either damage it or steal from it. For at least five years the roof, which had been completely stripped of its valuable tiles, was a landmark beneath its protective shroud of bright blue polythene. There was talk of demolition, as there always seems to be in Sheffield. It is a very permanent method of concealing incompetence. It is now a Grade II Listed Building.

However, private money was found, partly from two members of Def Leppard, the locally born rock group, Joe Elliott and Rick Savage, and the sad old school was transformed into a place with far more transatlantic influence than anywhere else in the city. The ideas used to achieve this change owe much to The Hard Rock Cafe and Planet Hollywood. I suppose it could be called an American theme bar and frankly it is a little too rich for me. Like it or lump it, it is better than letting it disappear. Many people have memories of this old school.

Since I wrote the above description of Players, it has closed down due to "financial" problems. By the time this book is published two things will have happened. Either it will have re-opened under a new and enthusiastic owner or it will be sadly once again derelict and ripe for vandalism!

The Deep End, Langsett Road, Hillsborough

Built between 1924-6 as a public baths, not just for recreational swimming, but with slipper baths for the use of the many residents of Hillsborough who lived in houses without a bathroom, it was designed in what has been described as a "robust Baroque style" by the city architect, F Edwards. It closed at the end of the 1980's and served its customary period of dereliction before it was converted into its new role.

Its style has been described as eclectic and innovative. A number of the original design features have been retained such as converting the changing booths into cosy little drinking corners. One of the big draws are the regular live music nights where it is encouraged to bring and play your own instrument.

Legends Cafe Sport, Langsett Road, Hillsborough

The name of this small, but beautifully made place is described well in its name. It is almost opposite The Deep, it used to be a Timpson's shoe shop and probably fits the bill as a warm up place before the big plunge.

The Walkabout, West Street / Carver Street

Many of the old die-hard Methodists, who used to dominate the Sheffield Magistrates Licensing Bench in the "good old days", must be turning in their graves at this latest addition to Sheffield's night life. I remember one notable New Year's Eve, not too long ago either, when this body of narrow minded bigots actually refused to allow the public houses in the fourth largest city in Great Britain to open until midnight! That decision must have marked the absolute peak of their huge and varied collection of old fashioned and woolly minded rulings!

For many years the Carver Street Methodist Chapel has stood empty, unloved and slowly disintegrating. Recently, it has had money poured into it and, since November, 1999, it is now an Australian theme pub. I probably won't ever visit it, but I must support the preservation of this grim old building. Okay, so it sells strong drink. Would any logical thinking person prefer it to be pulled down? On second thoughts, I might pop in and try one of the kangaroo burgers!

The Rat & Parrot, West Street

This cafe / bar is almost adjacent to Edwards, is composed of two floors and makes use of the building which, for many years, was the home of Andrews Graphics, who supplied artists materials. Again, an addition to the West Street "circuit". I wonder, in ten years time, how many places like this will still be in business?

Edwards, West Street

This, rather uniquely, is connected to The Old Red Lion, which has stood on its site for a great many years and which used, at one time, to be connected with the once noble art of boxing. It was at one time kept by Edward Platts, who was the father of the Sheffield heavyweight boxer, "Gus" Platts. Another boxer who had connections with this pub was Harvey Flood, a lightweight, who was landlord after he retired. He also, at one time or another, kept The Raven, Fitzwilliam Street (known as The Hornblower and now O'Hagen's) and The Harp Tavern, St. Phillip's Road.

Edwards is in the building which was originally W. Northends Printers Ltd. It was converted into licenced premises in the late 1980's and called Barkers. It consists mainly of one large bar-room and is merely yet another modern addition to the West Street young drinkers "circuit".

The Cavendish, West Street

This place is strictly a "fun palace" for those young people who still have to enliven a night out with the help of quiz nights, games machines, comedy nights, karaoke, very loud music and other intellectual pursuits. Formerly, I believe, a garage, it is now still a place which takes lots of money off its customers!

The name has been taken, with permission I am sure, from the Dukes of Devonshire, whose family name it is.

T P Woods, Leopold Street

Since the Grand Hotel was demolished in the 1970's, there have been various uses for this building. I think that before it became what it is today, it was actually a post office for a number of years.

This is a pleasant cafe / bar which has only been open since 1998 and is slightly less youth orientated than many of its peers in the city centre.

There will be other "premises" in the city that I have left out, or whose existence wasn't even thought of when I wrote this book. I am sure it won't both you - it surely doesn't bother me, as I very rarely go into any of them. The reason for this is purely and simply because they are not places frequented by middle aged men. They were never meant to be. We have our places where we go, young people have theirs. Eventually, when us "wrinklies" die off, the young people of today will take our places and the new youth, with its strange dress and even stranger habits, will take their places. Such is the way of things.

> *Omnia mutantur, nos et mutamur in illis.*
> *All things change, and we change in them.*

I nearly included The Surrey on Surrey Street, the former Masonic Hall and for a short period the registry office, but remembered that I included it in the first volume.

I did the same with the Rattener's Rest, but that closed a couple of years ago. It was a good idea; it was in the wrong place. It was no loss. Any pub which sells beer as awful as that place used to deserves not only to be closed down, but then burnt down and the ashes thrown to the four winds! I can get very bitter at times.

last orders

CHAPTER THREE
OLD PUBS WITH NEW NAMES

In the introduction I have already mentioned the alterations of pub names from perfectly sound, historically based names to modern "jokey" names. I believe that it's a passing phase. It appeared on the scene quickly; let's hope that it disappears with the same speed.

Just as a matter of interest, now that I am into a short chapter which is devoted to changes in the names of public houses, according to The Inn Sign Society, who are a collection of serious anoraks, the list of the Top Ten public house names in Great Britain is as follows:-

1 - The Red Lion

2 - The Crown

3 - The Royal Oak

4 - The Swan

5 - The Bell

6 - The Plough

7 - The White Hart

8 - The New Inn

9 - The King's Arms / The King's Head

10 - The Coach and Horses

Out of all these names, I think that Sheffield has at least one of each still open, except perhaps The Swan and The Bell. There used to be a Bell in Fitzalan Square. This closed in 1974 and is now a shop. The White Swan which stood on Meadowhall Road was demolished in 1998 and already the corner site has sprouted a small block of offices. On the corner of this stern, red brick pub there was a large mosaic of a white swan. I hope that the builders had the wit to save it. It would have been tragic to destroy such a treasure.

There are three pubs in the following list which have "Firkin" in their names. All three were once called something more traditional. These were all owned by Allied Domecq, which was taken over in the summer of 1999 by Punch Taverns. This huge group, at the time of writing, owns a chain of various types and styles of licenced premises, including Big Steak, Scruffy Murphy's and Tetley's, totalling around 3,500 pubs. Big as this estate is, it isn't the largest pub owning company in Great Britain. This honour goes to the Japanese banking giant, Nomura Investments, whose Grand Pub Company owns 5,000 outlets. Nomura is seriously wealthy and it has been estimated that it makes more money than both Toyota and

Honda. In 1997, it purchased the William Hill betting organisation. This information could well be out of date by now! The really big pub companies seem to swap blocks of public houses like gambling chips. This is why I have not mentioned the owners of the pubs listed in the later chapters.

For anyone who is really interested, a firkin is a beer cask which traditionally holds nine gallons, or half a kilderkin. A hogshead holds just over 54 gallons and a tun holds 210 gallons. So there!

The following is a selection of the pubs which have changed their names. There may be some others. The original name is listed first.

Nottingham House, Witham Road - Fitzooth & Firkin

Beehive, West Street - Foundry & Firkin

Woodseats Hotel, Chesterfield Road - Floozy & Firkin - recently reverted to its orignal name.

York Hotel, Fulwood Road - O'Neil's Irish Bar

Wig & Pen, Campo Lane - Shenanigan's

Mail Coach, West Street - Scruffy Murphy's

Hornblower (formerly The Raven), Fitzwilliam Street - O'Hagan's

West Street Hotel, West Street - Flares

Prince of Wales, Division Street - Frog & Parrot

Foresters, Division Street - Yorick

Dove & Rainbow, Hartshead - Tut & Shive (now reverted to original name 1999)

Old Crown, Scotland Street - R & B's Uptown Bar (now reverted to original name)

Museum, Orchard Street - Orchard then Brewing Trough now Hogshead

Hind (formerly The Nelson), Furnival Street - Seamus O'Donnell's

Norfolk Arms, Suffolk Road - Dodger's

Wellington, Henry Street - Cask and Cutler

Carlisle Street Hotel, Carlisle Street - Madison Bar

Norfolk Arms, Carlisle Street - Club Lukas or Club Xes

Cross Guns Hotel, Sharrow Lane - Tuxedoblue

Alma Hotel, Alma Street -
Now the Fat Cat

White Hart, Russell Street -
Kelham Island Tavern
Now closed

Roebuck, Charles Street - Newt & Chambers now Emporium

Old Blue Bell, High Street - Cavell's Bar

Royal Oak, Cemetery Road - Beer Engine

Bull & Mouth, Waingate - Boulogne Mouth then Tap & Spile now Tap & Barrel

Railway, Broughton Lane - Stadium now Noose & Gibbet

Albion, Ellesmere Road - Golden Perch, now Mill Inn or Tavern

Shakespeare, Bradfield, Hillsborough - Shakey's

Bassett, Cowper Avenue, Foxhill - Circus Tavern

Tankard, Stocks Hill, Ecclesfield - Stocks

Midland Hotel, Burncross Road, Chapeltown - Carousel

Wagon & Horses, Market Place, Chapeltown - Scandals

Coach & Horses, Manchester Road, Stocksbridge - Goodfellas

White Hart, St Phillip's Road - Paddy Maloney's

The Wellington, Langsett Road - Hillsborough Hotel

Fraternity House, the old TSB building on Norfolk Street, is now the Old Monk.

There are others, there are bound to be......

Finally, for this chapter, I have included a pub which is becoming extremely popular especially with CAMRA members, as well as others. This is The Hillsborough Hotel, 56 Langsett Road. It inhabits the corner site premises of the former Wellington Inn - indeed that name can still be seen above the main entrance door, but that is where any similarity with the previous public house ends.

This is a class or two, at least, above that doomed pub, which during its last few miserable years slipped well below the level of acceptability expected of licensed premises. It was no loss to anyone when it closed for business.

The building was bought by Del Tilling in August, 1998. After a good deal of work and financial outlay, including a complete internal refurbishment, it was reopened as a residential hotel and public house in May 1999.

Residents have the use of six en-suite bedrooms, benefit from indoor carparking and it has an English Tourists Board Two Star Rating. The popular public bar, which opens at 5pm, Thursdays to Saturdays, has already received a CAMRA award and always has eight assorted real ales on tap.

As a P.S. at the end of this chapter, especially for Real Ale buffs, who don't already know about it, there is in Sheffield a popular circuit of real ale pubs. These are:- The Fat Cat; The Gardener's Rest; The Cask and Cutler; The New Barrack Tavern; and The Hillsborough Hotel! Try it. You may discover a new type of hangover!

CHAPTER FOUR
SOME OLD NORTHERN PUB GAMES

As with many things, customs and habits, pub games are, or regretfully to a large extent were, very much a regional thing. A game popular in say the west of England could well have been completely unknown in the north east of England. It wasn't a bad thing; it helped to give each area of the country its own particular regional flavour.

It is a terrible shame that so many of these old pub games are dying out, especially the outdoor ones. Many pubs in bygone years relied on them to fetch in the extra customers which made the difference between a good living and scratching a living. From a business point of view, a team based at a pub was good news and money in the till for the landlord - players like to drink as do the spectators. This was helped by the fact that before TV became the entertainment god and cars spread the wings of the customers, the pub provided not only drink but just about all the diversion there was. This decline in interest is one of the reasons that the two most popular outdoor pub games in the north of England are becoming difficult to find.

Bowls, once a village institution, is still very popular, but has almost disappeared as a pub game and except for a few isolated examples, the pub bowling greens have gone. The reasons aren't difficult to work out and lack of space is probably the main one. A

Crown Green Bowling in the early 1900s

bowling green takes up a large lump of what may be a fairly small pub site and the temptation to put the comfort of the customers' cars first rather than that of a few bowls players has proved to be irresistible. Hence the tarmac is laid down and another green becomes a carpark.

Maintenance is undoubtedly the other main reason for the demise of the pub bowling green. It needs cutting, weeding, feeding, rolling and watering. In short, it takes dedication to produce and keep a perfect green. Sadly, this has not been forthcoming, so the green becomes a mess, so it is not used. It becomes overgrown and derelict. The excuse is there. Bingo. Another carpark is born!

Here in the north of England, of the two main bowling codes, the crown green game has always been the most favoured. It seems to me to be a slightly simpler and less formal game than its cousin, the flat green. Only two woods and a jack is needed; the jack length can be set at any distance and in any direction fancied across the slightly domed green surface. Perhaps this flexibility of the approach to bowling gives a small hint as to the attitude of Northerners to life.

I know of a large number of pubs in the city were there used to be a bowling green, but not many now that I can recall still have one in use. The Wadsley Jack, Wadsley Village is one and another is The Abbey, Abbey Lane. The third one that I know of is The Halfway House, Darnall Road. For this they are to be commended.

Knur & Spell team, Royal Hotel, Dungworth

The other outdoor game and one which is even harder to find is knur and spell. I have been told that it is still played in north and west Yorkshire and further north, although not nearly to the extent that it once was. Here in South Yorkshire it has disappeared, except in the memories of old men. Having said this, I may receive irate letters telling me that I'm wrong. I hope so, but I don't think so.

Let me explain something of this ancient game. The knur is what the player struck. It was originally a wooden ball, roughly carved by hand and made out of just about any type of wood, although I have read that boxwood, alder and apple woods were much favoured. These home-made balls had the slightly dimpled appearance of early golf balls, a game with which knur and spell is sometimes compared.

Some knurs were carved from horn and weighted with lead and, as the game developed, from the very hard and close grained wood, Lignum Vitae. As this wood comes mainly from the West Indies, it must have been both scarce and expensive. As his knurs were a source of great pride to most players, perhaps the expense was considered well worth it.

In the late 18th and early 19th centuries wood was mostly abandoned in some areas in favour of pottery knurs. These were handrolled from china clay and then baked at a very high temperature. I have read that they were about an inch and a half in diameter and weighed about an ounce. I saw one in Bradfield Council Offices and it was only about three quarters of an inch in diameter, so I expect sizes differed in different areas. These were known as "potties", hence the games' nickname "potty rise" in some areas of Sheffield. The Kelham Island Industrial Museum, in its Victorian life exhibition, has a steel spell and a collection of pot and clay knurs which are of all sizes.

The bat used to hit the knur was called the pommel or pummel. This had a shaft of between two and six feet in length. This length depended on the skill and preference of the player. It was made of wood, either ash, alder or hickory.

Onto the shaft was spliced the serious part - the striking face or buckhead. This could vary slightly in width - narrower for a long shot, wider for a safe, but shorter shot. The buckhead was made in two parts. The back piece was made of beech or a similar wood and glued onto this was the face. This most important part of the pummel was often, if available, made from old pit timbers which had already be subjected to great and prolonged pressure and were thus very dense. This wood was ideal. In non-mining areas, the wood was left for as long as possible in a metal press. After cutting to size, the wood was subjected to heat treatment from a blow lamp or similar. The length of this treatment had an important effect on the head. Prolonged heat produced a very hard head which would result in a long shot in calm conditions; a less tough head, produced by less heat, would work better on windy days and allow a slower, drifting shot to be played. This would take advantage of the wind. All very technical. The better, more serious players always brought a choice of pummels with them to a match.

The final piece of equipment needed to play this game was the spell. When, many years ago, the game first began to be played, the knur was usually propelled into the air by means of a flat board which was balanced on a peg driven into the ground. The knur was placed on the lower end of the board and the upper end was struck by the pummel. This threw the knur up into the air and the player hit it.

This simple and rather crude method was replaced in the 18th century by a spring trap made of wrought iron or steel, which did the same thing to the knur, but which was made in such a way as to allow the player to adjust spring tension and so vary the height to which the knur was thrown up. These gadgets were usually made by the local blacksmith and once made would last long enough to become the museum pieces that some of them now are. Bradfield Council Offices, which has a fine collection of local records, also has an old spell. This is rusty and damaged, but still looks as though it could be used today - except that no-one in Bradfield plays the game anymore!

These steel traps, or spells, were steadily replaced in the 20th century by the pin, which was cheaper to make and easier to use. This was merely a small gallows secured into the ground. From the crossbar of this hung a cord with an adjustable loop at the bottom end. This loop held the knur. When conditions were really windy, a piece of wire could be used to stiffen the cord.

There were two ways of scoring at knur and spell and both used the "score" ie. 20 yards, as the measuring division.

Long knock or striking involved any number of players and the winner was simply the player who hit the knur the longest distance. Many truly vast lengths have been recorded. Fred Moore of Halifax, playing in 1899, hit a shot of 18 score, 12 yards and one foot. Put another way, his knur travelled 372 yards and a bit. This was at a time when a distance of 12 score was usually long enough to win a match! A modern distance which won the world championship in 1970 doesn't compare very well. At The Spring Rock Hotel, Greetland, Colin Greenfield won with a knock of 10 score and five yards (205 yards)

The second way of playing knur and spell was known as scores or laiking. This was played between two contestants and each player had the same number of "cuts" or swings at the knur. This number was agreed before hand and could be as many as 30 or more. Each shot, taken turn about, was measured only in scores and fractions were ignored. So, if a player hit his knur and it landed between 160 and 180 yards from the spell, then he was credited with an 8 score. The player with the highest aggregate score at the end of the agreed number of cuts was the winner. Simple, huh?

These matches were serious affairs and there was a great deal of equally serious betting on the results. This, of course, sometimes led to "iffy" practices. The "doggers", whose job it was to mark each knur as it landed, weren't above treading an opponents knur into the ground so that it couldn't be found. Five minutes was usually allowed to search for lost knurs and after that time had elapsed, if it hadn't been found, then it declared lost and the player was awarded a nil score. Nothing changes much, does it?

I think that part of the reason for the decline in this grand old game is the simple fact that the large areas of clear, level ground needed to stage a match are becoming harder to find as towns and cities expand. Another victim of urban sprawl.

There used to be a childrens game called "peggy" fifty or so years ago, which was very popular. This was, to all intents and purposes, knur and spell for kids - or was knur and spell peggy for adults? I wonder what happened to it?

Thankfully, there are still indoor pub games which have survived. Darts, dominos, cribbage and the relative newcomer, pool, will probably always be around. In Sheffield there are still pub leagues which play either one of these games or a combination of them.

One game which used to be played at least in The Old Harrow, Main Street, Grenoside, was very simple. It merely consisted of throwing empty match boxes onto the narrow public bar mantelpiece. The winner was the player who managed to get the most boxes to stay there. Boxes which overlapped the edge didn't count. It was taken very seriously to the extent that money often changed hands after a game. And why not?

CHAPTER FIVE
GRENOSIDE

Before I begin to write about the villages surrounding Sheffield and their pubs, I should like to make a point or two about the various pub names that will be included in these following chapters.

These villages were once rural places, country communities. They were separated from each other and so were to a large extent self sufficient entities. The population was usually numbered in the low hundreds, so everyone knew each other; families married into families and not many people travelled very far. Where would they go and what would they do when they got there? Most of the inhabitants were uneducated people who worked with their hands.

This meant that agriculture played a large part in their lives. Sure, there were, from early in the middle ages, plenty of cottage industries involving the manufacture of articles which were needed by fellow villagers - edge tools, nails, clogs, brushes, etc., but the basic economic centre was almost always the farms. This was the longest surviving industry. Men have farmed the land and raised animals for many thousands of years. Long before the other industries arrived.

This rural base is reflected in the pub names. Here, in the outlying villages which surround Sheffield, as villages do around all large towns and cities, can be found names of pubs which reek of the countryside and which are not often found within the boundaries of towns and cities.

The Plough is one popular name which occurs regularly. This tool was regarded in the old days as far more than just a wooden or iron implement used for cultivating the fields. It was a symbol which was blessed and decorated, almost worshipped, on the Sunday or Monday which followed the winter break marked by the twelve days of Christmas. Don't forget that it is only fairly recently, in historical terms, that Christmas has been called that and regarded as a Christian festival.

Another rural pub sign is The Waggon (Wagon) & Horses. This is often seen as The Coach & Horses, although the latter name was usually only seen either beside or near a turnpike road. Pubs with this name, or sometimes The Hammer & Pincers or the Blacksmith Arms, often had a smithy beside them for the convenience of travellers. This was often worked by the landlord as a secondary, or perhaps even as his primary source of income. Pubs situated beside the old packhorse routes would often take that name.

Several pubs to the north of Sheffield are called The Hare & Hounds. This, I believe, derives from the popular local sport of beagling, which was especially followed in Ecclesfield. This village, from the 19th century, supported its own pack of hounds. These mainly hunted on the Bradfield moorlands and nearby.

Other animal names, although not all, have connections with the cruel, but popular bloodsports which were commonplace in the past - The Black Bull to bull baiting; The White Bear to bear baiting. The Cock could refer to cock fighting, or else the name could have another basis. If the pub was situated at the bottom of a steep hill (as The Cock, Oughtibridge is), it was often the practice of the landlord to keep a dray horse which he hired out to carters or carriers who needed help in pulling a heavy load up the hill. This additional horse was harnessed in series with the existing team and often made all the difference as to whether the cart got to the top of the hill, or not. This was known as the "cock horse".

One of the very oldest pub signs found in the countryside, although not in this book, is The Green Man. This has connections with the spirit of fertility. Many of the villagers only paid to organised religion what lip service they were forced to do by the law. For preference, and usually out of sight of the eyes of anyone in authority, they followed the "old religion" of their ancestors, as many still do today. Call them pagans, call them heathens if you wish. I prefer to think of them as pre-Christians.

Small survivors of the festivals of this old religion still colour our lives today and are so common that they have been adopted by Christians as part of their religion. Maypole dancing and well dressing, also possibly morris and sword dancing, are examples.

Some pub signs which are popular and which turn up in both town and country are concerned with royalty and the aristocracy. Some signs give an indication of who was the most influential person or family in the neighbourhood. Sheffield, both town and country, has plenty of names with Norfolk in them and, in the north and northeast, the Earls of Wharncliffe have their share.

The village of Grenoside, perhaps because of its geographical position, is still one of the most complete and self-contained communities that remain around Sheffield. Squatting as it does on a high bluff, from many vantage points it is possible to view miles of the surrounding countryside as it spreads out in different directions. I doubt if this would have been possible in the "good old days" when Sheffield boasted a thriving, heavy industrial base. Smoke makes an excellent shroud!

The village was first recorded historically in about the 13th century when it was known as Gravenhou. This apparently means a quarried hillside and this seems about right, at least up to the beginning of the last century. Once, there were extensive sandstone and granite quarries near to the village and stone was taken from here to build such places as the main post office in Fitzalan Square, erected in c1910 and now recently closed, and Hillsborough Barracks, dating from c1850 and now mainly a supermarket.

Wood also played a large part in the economy of Grenoside and this was due to the many acres of woodland which lie to the north of the village.

Before the invention of plastics and the other man-made materials that we take for granted today, wood was used for a huge variety of things and in Grenoside, as in many other villages throughout the country, people made a good living from making such things as baskets, clogs, charcoal and many types of brushes and fencing. Wood was plentiful, it grew cheaply and it was easy to work with simple tools. What more could be asked?

Now, these woods are still there, largely intact, but they are no longer considered to be a source of raw material and the craft of the woodman is gone. They are wild and unmanaged and left to the wildlife and for the quiet enjoyment of walkers.

The pubs which follow are mainly in two groups - those based on Main Street and those down on the Penistone Road. All are at least of 19th century vintage.

The Red Lion, Penistone Road

Known locally as "The Bottom Red", this pub has been much rebuilt since it first opened in the early 19th century. It was probably first developed as an inn to provide refreshments and stabling facilities for the travellers along the turnpike road which was opened in 1822 to replace the old road which ran along what is now Main Street from 1770. This new road was deemed necessary to avoid the long and tiring drag up Foxhill Road, a couple of miles nearer to Sheffield.

On the O.S. Map of 1850, The Red Lion is shown as The Old Red Lion; by 1890, it was known by its modern name. An early landlord was Thomas Ogden, 1849. It is not mentioned in the early 19th century trade directories. This could be because it was then only a beer-house.

The Blacksmith's Arms, Blacksmith Lane

There used to be a pub with this name somewhere in the vicinity of Blacksmith Lane. It is mentioned in the 1925 trade directory when it was kept by Enoch Marsh, who was by trade a blacksmith. A slightly later landlord was John Barker, 1933.

55

George French c1910

It is very possible that this was a short-lived beer-house almost at the junction with Penistone Road. This would make sense as passing trade along the turnpike would make the smithy viable. I have asked around the area and looked very closely at the buildings that are in Blacksmith Lane now and there is no sign of where a smithy or pub might have been. A vaguely possible site could have been on the corner of the lane which now serves as part of The Red Lion carpark.

A Chapeltown & High Green Archive Publication, " Ecclesfield Parish: People and Places", tells about a family named French who were blacksmiths working for four generations in the area. The first Mr French, who was born in 1802 in Eckington, married a Grenoside girl, Ann Tingle, and moved to the village to set up his blacksmiths business. He is recorded as living in Grenoside and working at his trade in 1841.

His son, Thomas, worked with his father as a blacksmith, having probably served his apprenticeship at his father's forge. He in turn trained up four sons. One of these sons, Frank, worked later from a smithy at Charlton Clough, off Bracken Hill, where he was assisted by his son, Walter.

The latest date recorded for a working blacksmith in Grenoside is 1910, but it can be fairly assumed that there was a smith in the village later than that date. The wrought iron railings which enclose the village war memorial, which stands at the junction of Penistone Road and Norfolk Hill and which records the dead from the village during two world wars, were made by Arthur French in 1920. This was at a time when the backbone of the blacksmiths trade, the horse, was fading into extinction and any blacksmith who wished to remain in business was forced to broaden his skills to general smithing.

The Norfolk Arms, Penistone Road

This solidly square, detached building has been little altered outside since its opening in the early 19th century beside the turnpike road. At one time it had a fine set of stables, but over the years, unwanted, these have gone. The rear windows offer a wide view over the Don Valley towards Rotherham.

19th century view

An early landlord was James Helliwell, who was also a timber dealer. This would have involved the wood which was harvested from the nearby Greno and Wheata Woods. He was there in 1833. A landlady, Ann Helliwell, probably his widow, followed him and was there in 1849.

Modern View

The Cow & Calf, Skew Hill Lane

Of all the public houses in Grenoside, this is the newcomer. It was opened in the early 1980's having been made from a collection of ancient farm buildings formerly known as Cross Hill Farm. This farm had been in the possession of the Smith family for many generations. It is now owned by Samuel Smith's Tadcaster Brewery. Modern breweries amuse and infuriate me. The majority of them care little or nothing about the history of the pubs they own, especially if they have just taken them over from another brewery, except when it pays them as an advertising ploy. But when they create a pub from some old farm buildings and turn them into a modern, moneymaking business, they still insist in giving it an "olde worlde" type of country name. They run a tight, well organised and expensive to enter alcohol vending unit and try to give the impression that it is a 19th century country pub. All that they can't buy to put in the bar is a group of straw chewing yokels. Perhaps they are already working on this!

The Angel, Main Street

The land on which this pub was built was apportioned under the Enclosure Act of 1789 and from that date until c1833, it was known as The Hammer & Pincers. This

seems to indicate that here, or very near to here, was situated a forge used by the blacksmith and farrier whose services would often have been in demand by the travellers using the original Sheffield to Halifax turnpike. This passed the pub along what is now known as Main Street until it was moved to the Penistone Road down the hill.

The name of this pub, The Angel, in common with similarly named pubs throughout the country, can be from one of two sources. Either it was the religious angel; or it was taken from the old English coin of the 18th/19th centuries, which was known as "an angel". This was from the design of an angel on one of its faces.

Early landlords included John Burkinshaw, 1833, and Charles Kay, 1841.

The Old Harrow, Main Street

This old pub, situated as it is in the centre of Grenoside, is one of the best documented public houses that I cover in

this book. In common with the adjacent Angel, this pub came into being following the Enclosures Act of 1789 when a man named Matthew Ellison was awarded one rood (about a quarter of an acre) and five perches (about five and a half yards) of land on the westward side of the Sheffield to Halifax turnpike. For this land he paid £9. This sounds really cheap using modern yardsticks, but this was at a time when farm workers were lucky to get two shillings a week in wages, so it wasn't that cheap. It did have a cottage and a garden on the site though. The cottage was later absorbed into the pub buildings when later extensions and alterations were carried out.

Matthew Ellison was an innkeeper, although not until 1802 was the "cottage or dwelling house" on the site first mentioned as being a public house. Then it was referred to as The Sign of the Harrow.

There follows here a fairly complicated passage about family deaths and inheritances. I like it; it makes a change to be able to follow closely the progress of a pub.

Mr Ellison, it is believed, died fairly soon after getting the land, leaving his property to his four offspring - Sarah, Elizabeth, David and George. Sarah died in 1796, followed soon by her sister, Elizabeth in 1800. George bought out his brother David's share of the property in 1802, but died soon afterwards in 1804 when the property passed to his two daughters, Ann and Mary.

Ann married Joseph Haigh and Mary married Joseph Woodhead - good, old Sheffield names! Woodhead bought out Haigh's share of the pub in 1823 and, when he died, the premises were inherited by Benjamin Woodhead, probably his son. Benjamin sold The Harrow in 1849 to George and William Walker Smith. Are you with me so far? I'm not going too fast, am I?

Although owners of the pub, these people don't seem to have actually run the place because in a trade directory of 1825, Mary Turner is recorded as being landlady. In 1833, William Croft was landlord, he was also a butcher. James Gillot, also a stone mason, was landlord in 1841 and in 1852, Thomas Lint was landlord. He came originally from Cudworth. Henry Bever, or Beever, was landlord in 1861 followed by Edward Marrison, or Morrison, in 1871. He also ran a horse bus service between the village and Sheffield. Nancy Nuttall was landlady in 1881, but by 1884 she had vacated the premises and they were being run by William Kirk.

Shortly after that date, William Heaps took over the licence. He was also a horse bus proprietor and the corner of the road at Main Street and Stephen Lane became known locally as "Heap's corner". Perhaps it still is. Following the death of Mr Heaps in 1898, his daughter's husband, Tom Wastney (or Wasteney), became landlord and when he passed away in 1901, his wife Phyllis, William Heap's daughter, took it over. When she remarried, her husband was licensee until he died in 1925. There is a butchers called Wasteney with a shop at the top of Norfolk Hill, opposite the pub. As this is a rather unusual surname, it seems likely that there is some family relationship here.

The Harrow was bought in 1896 by the Don Brewery, Penistone Road, Sheffield and this was the first time that this former free house had ever been tied to a brewery. As I wrote previously, the Don Brewery was taken over by Tennant Brothers and closed.

During the latter part of the 19th and early in the 20th century, The Harrow was probably the most popular pub in Grenoside. It had a lot going for it. There was a bowling green, a knur and spell team as well as a room upstairs which was used for dancing.

Talking of dancing, even in these all electronic and rather cynical days, there is still a group of sword dancers who perform outside the pub on Boxing Day each year. This is a custom which dates back many years.

The Harrow was extensively altered and internally refurbished in the 1980's and the premises were extended to include the small shop which has always been part of the main building. Today it is mostly just one huge lounge bar and something has gone from the pub - perhaps its feeling of history, perhaps its cosy, village pub atmosphere. It is the worse for that.

The Old Red Lion, Main Street

Usually referred to by the locals as The Top Red, this has, since the building was

converted from cottages, always been a public house. By this, I mean that it has never been an inn, although many people think that it was used as such for changing horses on vehicles using the turnpike road which once ran past it. I have never found any firm evidence to back this up, although until modernisation work removed them, there did use to be the remains of stables and the usual outbuildings which were associated with inns. In the 19th century and earlier, there was a distinct difference between public houses and inns. Today, there isn't.

The existing structure of the pub has been much altered internally, mostly during the 1970's and early 1980's. When I used to frequent the pub, it was made up of a maze of small rooms; now there is just one large bar as is the modern way. Many pubs were thus treated during that period. Evidence seems to suggest that it was once either two or three cottages dating from the middle of the 18th century.

The surname, Swift, has long associations with this pub. Joseph Swift was listed in the trade directories as landlord in 1841 and 1849. He was also a local quarry owned and the surname is well known in the village.

Quarries in the 19th century were a necessary and profitable business. Many of the workers in Sheffield, a large number of whom had recently arrived in the town during the industrial revolution, were needing at that time decently built stone cottages to live in and Grenoside had local stone in abundance.

Another Joseph Swift was listed as landlord in 1884, but by then the quarry connection wasn't mentioned. George Swift was landlord in both 1896 and 1901.

There is a story attached to The Old Red Lion concerning gambling. It may be true or it may be apocryphal. Before we had the 20th century luxury of betting offices, the police attitude towards this humble, but illegal activity was extremely strict. It was heavily frowned upon and a prison sentence was not thought too harsh a punishment for those who transgressed the gaming laws.

Men, of course, have always liked to gamble and in those days a man wanting to place a bet, unless he was actually at a race meeting, had to find a local illegal bookie or one of his runners. This wasn't very difficult in most towns, but in a small village it could pose problems. In Grenoside, the main calling place for the bookie was either The Old Red Lion or The Angel. This must have meant a payoff of some kind to the landlord, because by allowing gambling inside his premises he put his pub licence in jeopardy.

One day the bookie, who came from Oughtibridge, was sitting in The Old Red Lion when two men dressed like navvies came into the taproom where he was operating and ordered drinks. The bookie, with the sixth sense that he probably needed to keep him out of trouble, suspected that the two men were not all that they were supposed to be. He drank up and sidled off home.

When one of the supposed "navvies" asked one of the taproom loafers where he could get a bet on, as he had a "certainty" for one of the races the next day, he was told that he was too late and that the man had gone.

When they learned this, the two men asked which way the man had gone, so that they could catch him up and get a bet on. By now the man that they were questioning had twigged on that the two men were not what they seemed to be and could in fact be something to do with the law. As he had already served some time behind bars, he had no love for the police and directed the men down the road which lay behind the pub. This road led into the then dense woodland of Greno Woods, where strangers had been known to get lost for hours at a time.

The following day, at about five o'clock in the morning, the two men were seen staggering along Penistone Road, cold and wet, having spent a miserable night lost in the woods. I doubt if they were ever seen in Grenoside again. I've no doubt that life went on!

On an old map of Grenoside, dated 1850, there is marked a building named The Bird in Hand. This was not strictly within the environs of the village, but is placed along the Woodhead Road. This is the name taken by Main Street after it passes through Grenoside. I have searched for evidence of this building, but I have found nothing. It was very probably a small cottage, which became a beer-house for a short while to cash in on the trade passing along the road when it was a turnpike.

last orders

CHAPTER SIX
ECCLESFIELD

There are only three parishes left which are part of the Sheffield district. Ecclesfield is one of them, the other two are Bradfield and Stocksbridge, although the latter is actually styled a township.

The name of this ancient settlement of Ecclesfield probably comes from the Anglo-Saxon and means either church field or church clearing, for the village has boasted a place of worship since well before the Norman conquest. Then, the parish, far larger than it is today, was gifted to the Benedictine St. Wandrille's Abbey, Normandy. These French monks built the small priory in Ecclesfield which is today still partially intact. This priory was suppressed by Henry VIII and the church lands passed to the Earls of Shrewsbury and later, through marriage, to the Dukes of Norfolk.

St. Mary's Church, once known locally as The Minster of the Moors, was damaged and vandalised during the Civil War and almost all the internal fittings, and most importantly, the stained glass windows were destroyed. These were restored almost completely in the 19th century due to the efforts of the long serving and erudite vicar of Ecclesfield, Rev. Dr. Alfred Gatty, 1819 - 1903. He was the incumbent of the parish for 63 years and was also sub-dean of York Minster. He was probably the most powerful man in the parish at that time.

Unlike the adjacent villages of Chapeltown, Burncross and High Green, who relied largely on Newton, Chambers & Company, Ecclesfield has never had a major industrial concern to supply the work needed by the villagers, although no doubt many travelled the short distance to work for the company. This, however, mattered little in a village which had as far back as the 16th century, and possibly earlier, its own cottage industries which were devoted mostly to either nail making or file cutting with the odd cutlery workshop as well. This, together with farming and sending men down the nearby local coal mines, made for a prosperous and to a large extent self-sufficient community.

In common with many other men of past centuries, the file cutters and nail makers often doubled up their metal trade with farming in a small way and this need for a secondary income was a lifestyle shared with many pub landlords - the profits from a country beer-house could be meagre indeed.

When I was researching the village for snippets of interesting information to add to this chapter, I met Mr & Mrs Cooper, through their daughter, who works in the central library local studies section. Mrs Cooper is a member of the very old and numerous Ridge family, who have lived for many generations in Ecclesfield and its surrounding area.

The Coopers have spent many hours tracing the history of the Ridge family and I hoped, when I visited them, that they would reveal the identity and life story of an ancient ancestor who had, at the very least, been hung for sheep stealing! Alas, it was not to be - but what I learned was almost as good.

George Ridge, 1762 - 1839, was a yeoman farmer who had, at least, 15 surviving children. The fifth son was Thomas the Huntsman, who was a well known supporter of the Ecclesfield beagles pack and whose grave in the churchyard carries a verse extolling both his hunting prowess and his church going virtues. The second son was James and one of his sons was Robert, 1810 - 1891, and this is his story:-

Robert's life doesn't seem to have been anything out of the ordinary until he was 26 years old. This is when he had his first serious brush with the law.

According to a local newspaper, The Sheffield Register, later known as The Iris, dated March 9th, 1836, he appeared at York Assizes charged with what must have been grievous bodily harm in that he had been involved in a fight with another Ecclesfield man during which he inflicted a serious cut to the man's arm. This cut was so serious that the man later had to have the limb amputated. Robert was lucky because for some reason, either lack of evidence or witnesses, he was acquitted.

On his second appearance in court he wasn't so fortunate. The case was once again reported in the Sheffield Register, dated March 18th, 1843. I have taken from this report the bare facts of the case and as the newspaper didn't mention which court he attended, I have had to assume that he was once again at York Assizes.

This time he wasn't alone, but accompanied in the dock by John Hancock, George Storey and William Hall. They were jointly charged with burglary at Broomhill Toll House, near Rotherham on the night of March 8th, 1843. They were also charged with a similar burglary at the nearby Aldwarke Toll House on the same night.

The total haul from these two robberies was £6.12s.6d. The thefts had been effected thanks to the liberal use of cudgels carried by the men.

Although only these four men appeared in the dock during the case, it became evident that two other men had been involved. One was William Pressley, who turned Queen's Evidence and shopped his mates. This was either just to save his own neck or as well as that, for a share in the £150 reward which had been offered for the conviction of the culprits. The second man was Charles Fullalove, who either escaped or who for some reason was tried on his own.

An interesting fact was revealed in the newspaper report. Ridge was defended by a barrister named Sir Gregory Lewin. This man seems to have been a rather upmarket and expensive choice for a man prepared to risk the hangman's noose for a matter of a few shillings! As I have said, the total haul was only £6.12s.6d and as it was divided by six, then each man would have received about £1.2s (£1.10p). Big deal!

The men in the dock were convicted. His three associates received deportation sentences of 15 years apiece. Robert Ridge, considered perhaps as the ringleader of the men, received 20 years transportation. I think that considering the often very severe sentences handed down in those days, taking into account the fair amount of violence used during the crimes, the four men were lucky that they weren't hanged. Only 52 years before, Spence Broughton was hanged for simple highway robbery with no violence involved. His wretched body spent 25 years dangling from a gibbet on Attercliffe Common! Still, at least he had a road named after him!

It wasn't long before Ridge, in the company of about 200 fellow convicts, was on his way to the other side of the world. To spend the next 20 years, if he lived, of his life away from sunny Yorkshire. His destination was Norfolk Island. This penal colony, about 1,000 miles off the east coast of Australia, was an isolated and strictly disciplined place. It was where the hard cases went.

Ridge's stay, however, was fairly short, so he must have buckled down, accepted his lot and caused no trouble. He was then taken to Van Diemen's Land, an island off the southern tip of the Australian mainland. This today is known as Tasmania after the Dutch explorer, Abel Janszoon Tasman, 1603 - 1659. Tasman also discovered New Zealand.

I have no idea what sort of restrictions and disciplines were imposed upon these men who had been transported, but according to information found by Mr & Mrs Cooper, during the first few years of his confinement on Van Diemen's Land, Ridge became of all things, a policeman.

When, after being away from England for ten years, he received a conditional pardon, he could I suppose have returned to this country, but instead he stayed on and continued his police career. The date would now have been 1853/4.

He married in 1855 - the first of three wives he was to have in Australia, and the fourth overall if you count the one that he was believed to have married at sometime in Yorkshire! In 1857, while still a serving policeman, he entered the liquor business and became the landlord of The Garrick's Head, in Hobart, capital of Tasmania. It is very probable that this pub, many thousands of miles away from London, was named after David Garrick, 1717 - 1779, who was a famous, highly successful and versatile actor and theatre manager of the London stage. There is today, in London, a theatre named after him.

After serving in the police force for 21 years, Ridge retired but remained a pub landlord until his death. He is recorded in an Australian trade directory of 1881/2 as being the landlord of The Lennox Arms, Richmond. This was a town just outside Hobart. He would have been about 71 years old by then. The name of both this pub and the town would probably have had connections with the English Dukes of Richmond and Gordon, whose family name is Lennox. The Dukedom of Richmond was bestowed, in 1675, upon one of the bastard offspring of King Charles II, who did a lot of that sort of thing. The present duke is the 10th.

This wasn't, however, Robert Ridges's retirement home, as he is again mentioned in trade directories of 1886/7 and 1891, as being the landlord of The Denison Arms, Hobart. There is a pub of the same name in Sheffield. It is in Watery Street and at the moment boarded up. Both these pubs, on opposite sides of the globe, could well have been named after the family name of Lord Londesborough. I don't know why.

When Robert Ridge died, full of years at the age of 81 in c1891, he had been in Australia for 48 years and by any standards he had been a success. I can't help thinking what would have been the story of his life and would it have been so long and successful if, in 1843, he had been acquitted of the crime that he was charged with and not transported to Norfolk Island? I don't think that here, in South Yorkshire, in Ecclesfield, he would have achieved half as much as he did in what became his adopted country.

Ecclesfield has two rather unusual claims to fame. The Handbell Ringers are a well known and popular group of enthusiasts, which began its life in the early 1900's with a second hand set of bells bought from Grassington in Wharfedale. These were used by the group until c1925 when a new set were bought. This second set is known among the enthusiasts as a "long set" meaning that the set contains 170 bells. This is the set still used by the ringers. Still shiny

The Handbell Ringers have appeared several times on television. The last time was some 10 years back, when the BBC produced "Songs of Praise" from St Mary's Church.

The second unusual group are the Ecclesfield Beagles. These were founded in c1885 by the then owner and occupier of Whitley Hall, Thomas Bingley. Mr Bingley was a great follower of country sports and when, in 1912, it was decided for various reasons to move the beagle pack from the hall, he had new kennels built for the hounds in Townend Road. They have since moved from there, in 1987, away from the village to a more isolated country area on Wharncliffe Chase. The pack now numbers 20 couples of hounds, or in layman's language, 40 dogs.

The site of the original settlement of Ecclesfield, although it cannot today be considered the centre of the modern village, was around the area dominated by both the church of St. Mary's and, in those days, five pubs. The George & Dragon closed around the middle of the last century, but the remaining four are still thriving, although some buildings are different and a name has been changed. This is where the worshipping, the serious drinking and the rough, sometimes cruel, rural entertainment took place. Both bull and bear baiting were common up until the early part of the 19th century and this often took place in one corner of the churchyard where a set of stocks stand today.

The collection of public houses which still remain in the village must all be at least 100 years old, although the buildings that they inhabit may not be, and several must be a great deal older. Most of the pubs that follow are mentioned in the

1825/1833 editions of White's directory. I found it surprisingly hard work trying to find any particularly interesting facts about the pubs in Ecclesfield and the little that I did get is due to the knowledge of Cyril Slinn, who knows plenty about Ecclesfield. He was very liberal with his help and his time. I am indebted to him and also to Ted Earnshaw for his memories and Mr & Mrs Cooper for their patience.

The Griffin Inn, Town End Road

This pub was there in the early 19th century, but the present building is a Victorian replacement. It is built of Grenoside stone and Welsh slate. Some of the early landlords/ladies who kept the pub were: Elizabeth Butterworth, 1822; William Beard, 1833 and 1841, who also sold earthernware; Henry Froggatt, 1849; John Cox, 1852; John Gregory, 1877 and Robert Coward, 1901.

The White Bear, Stocks Hill

The old pub

This was mentioned in the 1825/1833/1841 directories when the landlord was William Unwin. He was followed by probably his widow, Lydia Unwin in 1849. The Unwin family had a unique link with the parish church of St. Mary's and were hereditary sextons. Many of the men in the Unwin family served in this capacity, many also kept the White Bear and many are buried in Ecclesfield churchyard.

Again, this is a replacement building. The earlier pub was housed in a smaller building behind the large, square pub which dominates the small square in front of it today. This first pub was included on the 1786 map of the village which was surveyed and drawn by Fairbanks.

I cannot offer any evidence to support it, but I believe that there is a very good chance that the name of this pub derives from the 18th and 19th century sport of bear baiting, which may well have taken place in front of the pub, as well as in the churchyard.

The new pub

The Tankard (or Olde Tankard), Stocks Hill

The name of this pub was changed fairly recently to The Stocks. The area over looked by the three pubs in this square used to be where the village stocks were situated. These stocks, which disappeared sometime during the middle part of the 19th century, c1852, are supposed to be the ones which are now in the churchyard, but to my jaundiced eye they appear to be too new to be the original ones. The Old Chapel, Whiteley Lane, Fulwood has an old set of stocks in the small front garden and these are far more worn and weather-beaten. They have obviously served their purpose many times.

The pub has recently been extended into a building already joined to it. This used to serve as the pub stables, until it became a garage. The pub now reaches the junction of Church Street and Stocks Hill.

Some 19th century landlords were John Roebuck, 1822; Richard Senior, 1833 and 1841; Benjamin Dixon, 1849; William Batty, 1852 and Charles Cook, 1877.

The Black Bull, Church Street

This pub directly faces St. Mary's Church and has an impressive frontage. It was

mentioned in the 1825 directory when the landlord was Aaron Ashton. This is not the original building. This was replaced in c1910.

For many years, and perhaps still today, local carols were sung in the bar at Christmas time. Today, this pub seems to be untouched by progress. It is still a collection of separate rooms, the decorations slightly grubby, the bar furniture old fashioned. There are dogs and wellington boots. It is the sort of place where no-one would turn a hair if a ferret's head popped out of a customers pocket. It is friendly and very like the pubs that I knew in my youth. It is a coutry pub and my favourite in Ecclesfield.

In 1833, the landlord was Matthew Jepson and in 1841, Matthew Joseph. Both these men were also coopers. Following them in 1849 was William Jepson.

The George & Dragon, Church Street

This used to face the junction of Church Street with Stocks Hill. The building is still standing and is divided into two shops. At the end of the building, on the corner, is a butchers shop. I'm not sure if that was ever part of the pub. It is not impossible that it was and that the landlord of the pub combined that with the trade of butcher. There are several such men listed in this book.

Above the window line of the former pub building can still be faintly seen the pub's name painted onto the masonry, although over the years this has almost disappeared.

It was listed in various trade directories and some former landlords/ladies were:- Sarah Stringer, 1822; Matthew Stringer, between 1825 and 1852, possibly a relative of Sarah - her son, perhaps. Matthew was also parish clerk of Ecclesfield. This position may have run in the family in the same way that the Unwins' were sextons. Esau Lee, 1877 and Arthur Mitchell, 1901.

The Arundel, The Common

This used to have the local cinema beside it, The Cinema House. This was built in 1920 as a privately funded local cinema venture. It was demolished in the 1960's, probably due to lack of custom.

The pub dates back to the beginning of the 19th century, but I have been unable to find much mention of it in trade directories until after 1841. This probably means that it was merely a small beer-house. The buildings give the impression of once being farm buildings. A single block with the farmhouse at one end and a barn at the other. This is born out by the part which looks as though it once was a barn used to have a pigeon cote built into one end.

One family, the Peppers', were long standing landlords of this pub. Various members were the licensees from c1893 until 1955.

The Traveller's Inn, The Common

This is another pub mentioned in the 1825 directory. It stands next to the building which once was one of the local blacksmiths. It could be that these two buildings were once connected. The detached building is of solid local stone and is a typical modernised old pub, although I suspect that it is not the original building.

It was kept in 1825 by George Bower, who seems to have been followed by his widow, Abigail. She was landlady in 1833. By 1841, the landlord was William Morrell.

The Ball Inn, High Street

A long serving landlord of this pub, who is mentioned in both the 1825 and 1841 directories, was William Yelland. He was also a well known local cattle dealer and it is likely that a small cattle market was held in front of or near to his pub.

After Mr Yelland, although not immediately, his widow, Mary, was landlady for a spell. The pub was then run for 80 years or so by a branch of the Ridge family.

Alfred Ridge, c1826-1882, was a filecutter by trade who became landlord of The Ball in 1876 or even rather earlier. After he died, in 1882, he left the pub in his will to his wife, Mary, on the condition that she didn't marry again. There is, however, reason to believe that she did so. There is no record of her keeping the pub herself, but it is difficult to believe that the pub left the family between 1882 and 1909 when her son, George, became landlord. George Ridge, 1857-1919 is recorded in a trade directory as being a greengrocer. He took over the pub in c1909 and ran it until he died there in 1919.

George's son, Alfred, 1888-1946, was landlord after his father's death until his own death. His wife, Stella, was the last of the Ridge family to run the pub. She left in 1957.

This is not the original pub building, but this present building is itself very old. Like the Arundel, it has the look about it of former farm buildings, but perhaps it is too near the centre of the village for this to be the case.

The Greyhound, High Street

Standing almost next door to The Ball, this is an older pub than its present building, which is late Victorian and rather ornate. There used to be a farmhouse and associated buildings on this site as far back the 18th century and when the pub was built, much of the original local stone was used. An extension was added to the pub in the early 20th century.

It is not mentioned in the 1825 trade directory. A former landlord of the pub, a Mr Kirk, was a keen rifleman and there used to be a private rifle range somewhere on the pub property. I have been told, but I have no evidence to back it up, that Mr Kirk also gave the money, which bought the first handbells owned by the Ecclesfield Handbell Ringers. An early landlord was George Dawson who was there between 1833 and 1849.

The Sportsman, High Street

Now demolished, this pub used to be approximately where the new and attractive local library now stands. Between 1825 and 1833 the landlord was William Foster. He was followed by John Lister in 1841 and 1849. Mr Lister was also a joiner by trade.

The High Greave, High Greave Road

This is a modern pub, but there has been a pub on this site for many years - as far back as 1841 and 1849, when the landlord was Robert Clitheroe.

The Plough Inn, junction of Church Street/Chapeltown Road

There used to be a pub, almost certainly a beer-house, which was in part of the building which used to be known as Coit Lane Farm - Coit Lane is now called Chapeltown Lane. I have been unable to find it mentioned in any trade directory and the only information I have got regarding this pub comes from an old Ecclesfield resident, Ted Earnshaw, who remembers it. After the pub shut, many years ago, the building was used for the storage of building materials. The building is now a private house with a builders yard attached. On part of the front wall of the house can be seen some very old wooden beams.

There is mentioned in the directory of 1825, a pub known as The Saracen's Head, but it has disappeared so completely that no-one knows even where it used to stand. All I know is that the landlady in 1825 was Elizabeth Butterworth.

CHAPTER SEVEN
CHAPELTOWN, BURNCROSS AND HIGH GREEN

Without plunging too deeply into the historical origins of this large, sprawling and only fairly recently heavily populated part of the north of Sheffield, I feel that a small outline about the industry which developed Chapeltown and its two neighbours into what they are today might be interesting.

Chapeltown first stopped being a small agricultural hamlet and began to make its mark with the building of an iron smelting furnace on the banks of the small local watercourse known as Blackburn Brook.

This initial industrial toehold was known as the Chapel Furnace and was probably operating as early as the 16th century. It was certainly a going concern in the first half of the 17th century. At the end of the following century, the Chapel Furnace went into decline due mainly to the opening of the Thorncliffe Ironworks further up the valley. This was the brainchild of two far sighted businessmen, George Newton, 1761-1825, and Thomas Chambers, 1745-1817. A good account of the careers of both men is to be found in Aspects of Sheffield I, edited by Mel Jones. What I am going to give is only the briefest outline as befits a book about pubs.

Thorncliffe Ironworks was built on land leased from Earl Fitzwilliam of Wentworth Woodhouse in 1793 and the company founded by Newton and Chambers became both one of the largest employers in Sheffield and a world famous name. It influenced almost everything which took place in the Chapeltown area even down to owning a company shop.

The industrial complex which was developed at Thorncliffe expanded as the company grew and thrived. It supported its own blast furnaces, four local collieries and various ironstone mines together with a complicated maze of railway sidings to handle the movement of raw materials in and finished products out. This was a vast change from the gentle meadows that had previously flanked the Blackburn Brook.

At its peak, probably around 1900, Newton, Chambers & Company employed over 8,000 workers, both men and women, girls and boys. These employees produced a huge and diverse range of products. These varied from railway lines to boot scrapers; forging hammers to bedsteads; clock weights to anvils. It seemed that there wasn't much, if it was made of ferrous metal, that the company couldn't make. One very popular and well known item was the Thorncliffe cast iron kitchen range - now much sought after by trendy house furnishers. Isn't it strange that an item once merely regarded as fit only for low grade scrap and destroyed in its thousands a generation ago, is in fact now being made again, at vast expense, as copies of the original?

One range of goods not made of metal, but produced from a by-product and which became a household name all over the civilised world, was the Izal range of germicidal disinfectant products. This was made from the oils and tars obtained during the conversion of coal into coke for use in the blast furnaces. These goods were first produced in the 1890's and was so little valued by the company that it was first marketed as a sheep dip and similar.

During the Second World War, an excavator factory was converted into a plant for manufacturing Churchill tanks for the Army and by the end of hostilities in 1945, 1,160 of these lumbering machines had clanked off the production lines. One is still left, as a monument, outside the plant which used to make them. It is now a transport company. Following a take-over in 1973, after 180 years of independent trading, the company was split up, reorganised and sold off as it suited the new owners. Some might call it asset stripping. A modern housing estate was built on the former site of the Izal Works and on

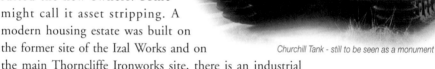

Churchill Tank - still to be seen as a monument

the main Thorncliffe Ironworks site, there is an industrial estate, although I believe that the original main office block used by Newton, Chambers is still standing.

Little is left now of Newton, Chambers & Company, apart from a memorial hall, various plaques on buildings scattered round the area, the graves of the founders.... and until June, 1999, a jokey pub name in Sheffield, The Newt & Chambers. Even this has now gone, changed to The Emporium!

I have outlined very minimally how Newton, Chambers & Company were a major influence on Chapeltown and its surrounding area, but there were, of course, other firms operating in the vicinity. Not so large, it is true, but still leaving their own imprint. Two who both disappeared in the 1980's were Parramore's Foundry, which began as brass founders and finished as mainly makers of cast iron products; and Charlton Ironworks, which also made cast iron products and were well known for both their kitchen ranges and mantelpieces.

Although, as in many areas of Sheffield, the serious industry has gone, the housing estates have not only remained, but have swelled and multiplied. The proportion here of pubs to head of population is excellent.

Although most of the following pubs are still open, unfortunately, for some reason, I have been unable to unearth much by way of interesting information about them. I could pad out my descriptions of them with my own opinions of them as pubs, but perhaps that is better left to the individual customers.

The Crossfield Tavern, Mortomley Lane, High Green

This is a pleasant roadside pub which is at the corner of a terrace of similar, granite built houses. It has been there since at least the beginning of the 19th century and in 1849, the landlord was William Parkin.

The Crown and Cushion, Chapel Road / Burncross Road, Chapeltown

During the Second World War, Queen Wilhelmina of the Netherlands was an occasional house guest at this pub. She came from London, where the Dutch royal family were living in exile, to visit the Dutch refugees who were living in a displaced persons camp shared with Polish evacuees. This camp was near Barnes Hall, the former family home of the once powerful Smith family.

The Crown Inn, Penistone Road, High Green

This is not in the village, but sits at the side of what was once the turnpike road to Halifax. It was built on ground owned by the Earl of Wharncliffe probably sometime in the late 18th or early

19th century. The basic building material was local granite from the quarries at nearby Grenoside creating a three storey building with, for some reason, an outside staircase to serve the top two floors. This is a building feature that I have never come across before.

In 1841, this pub was kept by Joshua Pearson; in 1849 and 1856, by Mark Yeardley, who handed over the running of the pub to his son, John. He was a small farmer working a holding of about 45 acres. In 1871, the census recorded that living in the pub were John Yeardley, his wife, six children and a married couple with two children who were lodgers. The male lodger, Charles Brownhill, was a coal miner, who would have worked at the now closed local collieries.

The inn in its early days was a free-house, as was common, and it was bought by Stones Brewery, Rutland Road, Sheffield. During this period of ownership it had

several landlords including the names Richmond, Moxon, Parker, Jakes and Maw.
In 1928, the brewery sold the pub to Maurice Weldon. Mr Weldon was followed, possibly on his death or retirement, by his daughter, Mrs Smith.

At one time, there was a clause in the pub lease which stated that the inn and its attendant land must not be separated and must be worked as a single enterprise. Whether this is still the case, I don't know. The pub is now once again a free-house.

The Rose Inn, Thompson Hill, High Green -

This pub dates back to 1849 and, unusually for the historic dating of public houses,

The Rose Inn before the First World War

this can be backed up by a lease. This used to be in existence, it was dated 1849 and ran for 99 years. It stated that the pub had only just been built. At that time, either the building or the land upon which it stood, or both, belonged to the Duke of Norfolk.

In 1871, Joseph Yeardley was the landlord. At the same time, John Yeardley, as mentioned earlier, was landlord of The Crown, Penistone Road. It seems likely that these two men were related in some way.

The Rose Inn was bought in March, 1889, by Smith, Redfearn & Company, Don Brewery, Penistone Road, Sheffield from J Redfearn. Again, there is a similarity in these names, but whether there was any family relationship between the seller and the buyers is not known.

This brewery began life in c1832, when the brewery buildings were erected. It was firstly known and traded as Turton, Warburton and Co; then as Howe and Smith's. In 1854, it began to trade as Smith, Redfearn and Hanger; later as AH Smith, Redfearn and finally as AH Smith and Company. This was a decent sized brewery who, in 1900, owned 83 public houses which had a market value of about £250,000.

It was swallowed up by Tennant Brothers Brewery in 1916. The new owners closed it as an active brewery. Until 1994, when roadworks forced the demolition of the remaining buildings, there used to be a rather dilapidated wine and cigar warehouse left on a site beside Penistone Road. On one side of this building, there was a plaster or cement logo with both the company name and the uses of the building on it. Before the building was razed, this was copied and a facsimile sign was later mounted in the wall beside the new road where it can be seen today. (see chapter one page 30).

Some early landlords of The Rose Inn were:- Joseph Thorpe, 1898; Francis Wildsmith, 1921-1929; Grace Wildsmith, his widow, 1929-1933; Hubert Mellor, 1933-1938; Cyril Bramley, 1938-1973.

Until 1947, the pub only held a beer-house licence. This was upgraded to sell wines as well after that date and in 1949, it gained a full public house licence.

The Bridge Inn, Lane End (just above Charlton Brook), High Green

This pub was closed in 1956 and all its buildings were demolished without trace to make way for a housing estate. It once had a beehive in its garden in the shape of a dolls house.

The Barrel, Lane End, High Green

This is directly opposite where The Bridge Inn used to stand. Charlton Brook runs

down the side of the pub and actually beneath a side extension. At the rear, there is a fine set of old buildings which could have been stables An early landlord of this pub was Joel Hobson, who presided over it in 1841 and 1849. The advert on the house was not on the wall of the pub. That was at the rear on the right.

The Bridge Inn, Hollow Gate, High Green

Standing in the bottom of a small valley which is followed by Charlton Brook, this pub is still open, although the small weir and reservoir which used to exist on the opposite side of the road have long been filled in. Charltonbrook Reservoir is still there, situated some way behind the pub and now well within the boundary of a housing development.

The Travellers Inn, Thompson Hill, High Green

There are a huge number of pubs with this name, many in Sheffield. There is one less now, however, as this pub is closed and is now a private house. It was part of a terrace of similar houses.

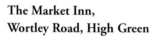

The Market Inn, Wortley Road, High Green

This is one of a group of pubs which cluster around what was once the market place in the centre of the village. High Green is now, however, just part of a conurbation with Chapeltown and Burncross.

There used to be a turnpike at this pub where travellers had to pay their toll when travelling between Rotherham and Wortley. Whether the landlord was the toll-keeper I don't know, but it seems likely that he would have been.

The Old Cart and Horses, Wortley Road, High Green

Dating back to the early 18th century, this could well be the oldest pub in High Green, and it bears one of the oldest country pub names. Inside it is cosy and has been preserved well. The original, or at least, some very old stables are still at the back of the building. Two early landlords were:- John Cartledge, 1841 and George Beardshall, 1849.

The Packhorse Inn, Packhorse Lane, High Green

This old pub stands at an ancient resting place on the "salt way", which ran from Cheshire, over the Pennines, to finish at Rotherham about six miles further on. It may seem to be rather near the destination to have a resting place, but six miles was a long way with a packhorse train, especially after walking from Cheshire and handling anything up to 50 heavily loaded packhorses.
An early landlord was James Parkin, 1849.

The Phoenix, Greengate Lane, High Green

The name of this pub, which is a fairly new, "estate" type pub, seems to suggest that there was an earlier pub on this site, but I have been unable to find any evidence for this.

The Pickwick, Packhorse Lane, High Green

This is a very modern pub cum club in a very functional building. Why it was felt necessary to call the place after a Dicken's character, I have no idea.

The Queen's Head Inn, Wortley Road, High Green

Dating back to early in the 19th century, in 1849 the landlord was John Walton. The queen whose head gives the pub its name must have been Victoria. She was the first queen to reign in this country since Queen Anne and the pub doesn't go back that far.

The Salutation Inn, Wortley Road, High Green

I haven't been able to find much information about this pub, except for the fact that in recent years the incumbent landlord was allegedly shot dead by his common law wife, the landlady. I think it was deemed as manslaughter.

This popular pub name, there have been several in Sheffield and a huge number spread over the country, has religious connections.

The White Hart, Wortley Road, High Green

This is a c1930's type of pub built almost on the site of a previous pub of the same name. The first pub was kept by Sarah Johnson in 1841. She was followed by William Kilner who was also by trade a butcher. It seemed to be fairly common to mix these two trades. This is a very common pub name and, I believe, it derives from the shield badge of King Richard II, 1367-1400. There is only one pub called the Red Hart in England and that is in Hitchin, Herts.

The Wharncliffe Arms, Burncross Road, Chapeltown

This 19th century pub is stone built and attractive. There is a stone over the front door which carries the date 1874. It takes its name from the local Earls of Wharncliffe, who have naturally many local pubs named after them. The family name of this branch of the British aristocracy, who were given an earldom in 1876, is Montague-Stuart-Wortley. The present incumbent is the 5th and is, I believe, from Australia. He owns little else apart from the title as the family home of the clan, which is in the village of Wortley, has been owned and used for many years by a trades union organisation. The previous earl was a former jazz drummer and later a garage owner. He survived a bad car crash and died in his 50's in 1987. He was what is usually called a "character".

The Prince of Wales, Burncross Road, Chapeltown

This small, detached pub still retains the traditional pub layout - a "best" bar and a "public" bar on either side of a central bar area. It is easy to imagine being deep in the countryside while inside, until you leave and find out that it stands on the side of a busy road in a built up area.

Probably named after the famous Prince of Wales who later became King George IV, 1762-1830. Although he had a European-wide reputation as a "playboy", he was also probably the only resident there has ever been on the throne of Great Britain who has actually shown any appreciation of art and architecture.

The Acorn, Burncross Road, Chapeltown

This pub is away from the clusters of pubs which mark this area. It is a stone built, detached building which gives the impression that it was once farm buildings, although it dates back as a pub to at least 1849 when the landlord was Thomas Chapman.

I have come across very few pubs with this name, but there have been several in Sheffield. The name could, rather tenuously, perhaps have some connection with King Charles II, who was reputed to have escaped capture after his defeat in the battle of Worcester, 1651, by hiding in an oak tree. Perhaps, perhaps not. In the summer, the flowers on display outside in hanging baskets are exceptional.

The Midland Hotel, Burncross Road, Chapeltown

Like The Waggon and Horses, this pub has adopted a "trendy" name, The Carousel. It is a large, detached building standing sideways to the road. It somehow gives the impression of being too large for the area, as if it had been designed for the centre of a town, rather than for the outskirts of a large village. It dates from the 19th century.

Bank at the front, pub in the background c1900

The Waggon and Horses, Market Place, Chapeltown

The name of this pub was changed to Scandals a number of years before changing pub names to attract the younger end of the drinking public became popular. Although I have never been in this pub, one of the few, I have a feeling that it aims to more of a night spot than a public house. This is a replacement building. The original pub was demolished c1920 and this large, detached building was erected.

Original Waggon & Horses pre 1920

It is mentioned in the 1825 trade directory when the landlord was James Barton. He was succeeded in 1833, by John Depledge who was followed in 1841 by his son, George.

The Coach and Horses, Station Road, Chapeltown

This is a comfortable country pub which stands sideways to the busy Station Road and is opposite The Royal Oak. In 1833, the landlord was G Hoyland; in 1841, Joseph Falding and in 1849, Joel Hague. Pubs with this name usually were situated on or very near to turnpikes.

The White Horse, Market Place, Chapeltown

This stood adjacent to the Waggon & Horses and slightly to the rear. It was believed to date from at least 1720 if the information on a date sign which used to be at the front of the building was correct.

In the trade directories of 1825 and 1841, the landlord is listed as Charles Hoyland who was also a butcher with a shop beside the pub. He was followed by his son, William who was landlord in 1849. The pub's name could be derived from the galloping white horse which was an heraldic device of the House of Hanover.

The last landlord was a Mr Kilner and he was there until 1914 when the inn lost its licence. The buildings, or replacement buildings, snuggling up to the railway bridge, were then shops until 1974, when they were demolished to make way for the ASDA supermarket which stands today.

The Royal Oak, Station Road, Chapeltown

Standing slightly back from the road, this pub stands beneath the shadow of the supermarket built on a site above it. Similar to The Coach and Horses in many ways. Both these pubs carry old and illustrious English pub names. Royal Oak pubs usually derive their names from the escape of King Charles II in 1651 following his defeat at the Battle of Worcester during the Civil War. He was alleged to have hidden in an oak tree to avoid his pursuers. This was the final battle during the civil war and victory here made Oliver Cromwell master of all Britain. Charles II was restored to the monachy in 1660.

The Commercial Hotel, Station Road, Chapeltown

Strangely, this pub is not mentioned on a map of 1905, although it was photographed in the early 1900's. This is possibly because it only held a beer-house license. The pub used to be directly opposite the old Izal factory owned by Newton, Chambers and must have relied on many customers from that source. During that time it would have prospered, but when the factory was demolished and a new housing estate was built on the site, the pub lost a large slice of its customer base. As a consequence, it began to slide and was perhaps heading for closure when the present incumbent, Paul Menzies, took it over.

After much hard work and investment, Paul has managed to create a rare gem of an establishment - a pub which serves real ale, much of which is brewed at The Wentworth Brewery, of which Paul as a director; good food and something else which is rare today, a relaxed and friendly atmosphere, which is not quite of the present day. I didn't miss the lager louts, or the canned music; I welcomed the pub layout and the ease with which the regulars chatted at the bar.

For the real ale buffs, the range of Wentworth Brewery beers sold in The Commercial and other pubs is thus:- Oatmeal Stout - 4.8%; WPA - 4% ; Venture - 3.6%; Best Bitter - 4.2%; Gryphon - 5.1% and the big one, Rampant Gryphon - 6.2%. There are always other real ales on tap, of course. The chapel which used to stand beside the pub was demolished fairly recently to make way for an access road to an elderly persons residential home.

The Miners Arms, Warren Lane, Chapeltown

This pub, probably because it was at that time a beer-house, is not marked on the 1905 map of the area. It is an attractive old building which gives the impression that it was the result of knocking together two or three workmens' cottages. It is next door to The Thorncliffe Arms.
Sheffield has had many small collieries, all of which are today closed, but it has never nursed as large a mining industry as has Barnsley, Wakefield and further north. There have been, in spite of this, a number of pubs with this name in the city.

The Railway Hotel (or Inn), White Lane

Now closed and a private residence, it stood beside the railway bridge. This bridge was first made out of wood which was later replaced by a steel one. This final bridge was demolished as redundant in 1975. The railway station itself closed in 1953.

The Norfolk Arms, White Lane, Chapeltown

This has been, over the last few years, extensively modernised and extended. Very recently, a motel bedroom block was added, which, when it was in its planning stages, caused an upheaval between the pub owners and the outraged local inhabitants. Unfortunately, as so often happens nowadays, the bad guys won!

The pub dates back to at least the middle of the 19th century when the landlord was James Almond and is the last pub in Chapeltown on the road to Barnsley.

This was one of the most popular and numerous pub names in Sheffield, and although many of them have closed down over the years, there are still plenty left.

The Thorncliffe Arms, Warren Lane, Chapeltown

This is equally as attractive as The Miners Arms and would have been very popular with the workers from, and was probably named after, the nearby Thorncliffe Ironworks.

During the period that a large number of navvies were working on constructing the nearby railway tunnel, it is said that to keep the two groups of workers apart, and thus save the pub from premature demolition, the navvies, mainly Irish, had a special room built for them. To go to these lengths must give some indication of their value in monetary terms to the landlord!

There used to be a pub called The Ball at Mortomley Lane End. I have no idea either where it actually was or when it closed, but I do know that the landlord in 1841 was Joseph Bennett.

last orders

CHAPTER EIGHT
STOCKSBRIDGE, DEEPCAR,
BOLSTERSTONE & LANGSETT

The township of Stocksbridge was, before the industrial revolution, a typically rural area clinging to the side of a river valley. After the arrival of Samuel Fox's steelworks in 1842, this village began to expand and thrive, developing the need for shops, schools, housing, roads and pubs. Without this steelworks and its offshoots, Stocksbridge and its immediate neighbour, Deepcar, would, I am sure, have remained for many more years nothing more than small, thinly populated country villages. They would have expanded eventually as the years passed, but it was the Fox company which began it and it was this company which was to wield so much influence in the area for at least the next 100 years and more.

There had been, before the steelworks arrived, pubs in both Stocksbridge and Deepcar, but these would have been mere beer-houses used to relying on the trade of the villagers and those who passed on the road to Manchester and beyond.

Bolsterstone and Langsett have remained rural areas, although inevitably they have been subjected to population increases as the housing estates have mushroomed and the use of motor vehicles brought the city of Sheffield closer.

Bolsterstone was described in a handbook for ramblers published in the early 1900's as being, "the most compactly grouped, clean little village that you ever saw." and it is still true today. The large church, hugely out of proportion to the size of the village, is well worth a visit. So is The Castle Inn, the headquarters of the world famous male voice choir.

There isn't a huge amount known about Langsett during the 18th and 19th centuries. This is believed to be due to the extremely short-sighted, and to my historically motivated mind, criminal action taken by a past landlord of The Rose and Crown pub.

This man, new to the public house and no doubt keen to make his mark, found two large wooden chests somewhere within the pub buildings. These are believed to have contained many old papers and documents, dating from the early 19th century and possibly before that, which recorded a great deal of information concerning the Manor of Langsett. How they got there is not known. He wanted to make use of the boxes for some other purpose, so he destroyed, probably by burning, all the contents. This has left a large gap in what we know about the village.

Langsett is a village dominated by its reservoir which was opened in 1905. During the time taken to build this, the small village must at times have seemed to be almost entirely populated by navvies.

Special housing was built for them together with a canteen and, of course, there would have been plenty of trade for the two pubs which existed then. Langsett can only boast the one pub now, The Waggon and Horses, but it does have a decent reservoir.

The Royal Oak Hotel, Manchester Road, Deepcar

This pub stands in the centre of the village near to the road junction which has tested the inventiveness of traffic light installers for many years. It can be dated back at least as far as 1860 and had generous stabling to the rear as would have been needed during the days when many horses used the Manchester Road.

The King and Miller, Manchester Road, Deepcar

Almost opposite The Royal Oak, this is another old pub probably dating from the 18th century. I suppose that it is possible for the name to be connected with the mill which used to stand on the other side of the road. In 1829, the landlord was James Green; he was followed in 1833 by Thomas Hague and then in 1841, George Grayson took over. The landlords seemed to have had a fairly short reign.

The Traveller's Inn, Vaughton Hill, Deepcar

This pub was known locally as "the low drop", because of its position as the lowest of the three properties built on the hill. It closed as a pub in 1920 and became a private house. In 1851, the landlord was named Vaughton, hence presumably Vaughton Hill. The landlord rented the premises from the Lord of the Manor and, for some reason, only paid a "peppercorn" rent. In 1833, a licence application records the landlord as being George Siddons.

At the bottom of Vaughton Hill, on the opposite side of the road to the pub, there used to be Deepcar Corn Mill which has long since been demolished. When it was there, it wouldn't have hurt the profits of the pub. Milling is a very dusty business!

The Friendship Hotel, Manchester Road, Stocksbridge

The most well known landlord of this pub was Tom Batty. The frontage today carries his initials together with the date 1903. This, I believe, doesn't indicate that a new pub was built then, rather that a new facade was built on the front. There used to be a bowling green to the rear and Mr Batty owned a field which he allowed the local football team to use. The pub used to be known as a "call office". This was because it had installed one of the newfangled telephones which was available for public use. There were also telephones in The Royal Oak, Deepcar and The Coach and Horses, Manchester Road, Stocksbridge. The landlady between 1868 and 1871 was Mrs Harriet Battye and in 1881, Elijah Askew.

The Sportsman's Arms, Haywoods

Mr and Mrs Pladdy ran this pub for 38 years. It was a meeting place for many local clubs and organisations. Thomas Pladdy was a well known local angler and his wife ran a soup kitchen during the 1926 general strike. They retired from the fray in 1949. The pub is now closed and is a private house.

The Coach and Horses, Manchester Road, Stocksbridge

The pub is dated from the early part of the 19th century and is still in business although a couple of years ago it changed its name to Goodfellas, I hope this is a short term name.

The Rising Sun, Hunshelf Bank, Stocksbridge

This pub was on the other side of the river valley overlooking Fox's works. It was probably a beer-house most, if not all, of its life.

The Dog and Partridge, Broadhill

The whereabouts of this pub is not known, although it is recorded as being open in 1833.

The Silver Fox, Manchester Road, Stocksbridge

Although the pub itself is too new to yield anything very interesting historically, the site upon which it is build is worth a few lines.

In c1774, the building then on this site was called How Fall and was a large farmhouse with associated outbuildings. It was called Hauve Hall almost 100 years later when it was recorded during the census of 1871.

Between 1851 and 1891, the Hattersley family were in occupation. James, the father, was followed by his son. Presumably they farmed the surrounding land. It is not known when the hall was demolished, but The Silver Fox was built about 35 years ago to serve the private housing estate upon which it stands, which was built at the same time. I wonder if the name is a pun taken from the name of the Samuel Fox steelworks.

The New Inn, Manchester Road, Stocksbridge

This old pub used to be one cottage in a terrace of similar cottages. Then it was known as The Corner Pin. Now, it has been extended into the adjacent building. It is still open as a free-house.

The Red Grouse, Spinkhill Lane, Stocksbridge

This is one of the rare Samuel Smith's public houses in this area. It still serves the council estate which was built at the same time.

The Miner's Arms, Bracken Moor Lane, Stocksbridge

This pub is nicknamed "the rag" or "rags". I have been told that this is because the workmen from the local gannister pit used to frequent the pub while still in their working clothes. Gannister, by the way, is a type of clay which is used for fire bricks in the steel industry. It is probably a lot cleaner today.

The Castle Inn, Bolsterstone

The landlady in c1907 was Mrs Ann Bramall; the previous landlord was her father-in-law, Thomas Henry Bramall. She bought the pub together with six "closes" of land in 1907 for £4,750. (A close of land is a small, enclosed field) Her father, Joseph Grayson of Leeke House, Haywoods was a coal merchant of some means. It is now famous for its association with the Bolsterstone Male Voice Choir.

The Broomhead Mill House, Ewden Valley, Bolsterstone

This was a public house until the landlord, George Staniforth, was killed, in c1855, following an argument over the result of a dog fight. The pub's licence was rescinded and the disgraced building was later demolished A replacement building was put up and this perished beneath the waters of the Broomhead Reservoir. End of story!

The Rose and Crown, Nether Midhope

This pub was situated on the Langsett / Wadsley road at the crossroads at Nether Midhope. It was built by William Payne of Frickley, near Doncaster. He was a very wealthy man, a Quaker and a property developer. He became Lord of the Manor of Langsett, when he reputedly bought the title from Lord Melbourne in 1802 for £116,400. I frankly don't believe this huge figure and believe that it has become distorted in the telling over the years. I feel that it should be either £11,640 or £1,164. Either of these sums of money would be large in those days

The pub was a coaching inn and was supposed to have had a ballroom on one of its upper floors. It closed on 25th May, 1876 and became, I think, Lower Hand Bank Farm.

The Waggon and Horses Inn, Langsett

Built by William Payne in 1809, it was of the same design as The Rose and Crown. At one time it was practically the only building in the village that wasn't owned by the Yorkshire Water Company, as it used to be known. It was always a free-house and was referred to as The Inn, Langsett until c1924-27. It is still open.

When the large, ugly, chapel like building was in the process of construction, it was only towards the end of the job that it was noticed that the apex of the gable, above the central window, was well out of line. This must have both irked and puzzled the builders. I know that it would have irked me!

There is, in trade directories, information about a Coach and Horses in Bolsterstone. The landlord in 1849 was William Wagstaff. Also about The Barrel in Bolsterstone. The landlord in 1841 was John Bramhall. I can't add to this information nor give the locations of these two mystery pubs.

last orders

CHAPTER NINE
HIGH AND LOW BRADFIELD

Stand as I have done in the monument crowded churchyard of the 15th century church of St. Nicholas, in the village of High Bradfield. Look out over the surrounding countryside and it is difficult to believe that only a handful of miles away lies one of the largest cities in England

Covering about 35,000 acres and reputedly the largest in the country, Bradfield Parish is studded with small villages and tiny hamlets; it has grouse; it has moorland fires. It is also a wild and thinly populated area stitched together roughly by narrow and serpentine roads. These have many stretches that have no place for anything larger or faster than a farm tractor. It is not hard to become lost in this tarmac maze and to follow the thin thread of a road for a mile or more only to finish up in a farmyard.

The Loxley Road, a link between Sheffield and Bradfield, is an exception. It leaves the urban closeness of the city at Malin Bridge and follows an almost arrow straight path along the Loxley Valley. At the Dam Flask reservoir, the road divides and swings left and right around the huge and silent stretch of the dam to finally finish up in Bradfield Parish.

What about the Bradfields' themselves? There are two of them - High and Low and they are within a mile of each other. High Bradfield, logically, is higher up the hill and is often referred to as simply Bradfield - I'm not sure which is correct. Not much of this parish is mentioned in that symbol of historic significance, The Domesday Book of 1086 - not the Bradfields, nor Stannington or Dungworth. Perhaps the surveyors of the ancient tome found the bleakness of these Yorkshire moors too intimidating for their French taste!

There were two main pubs in High Bradfield, although there were probably, as in all the scattered rural villages around Sheffield, a number of ale- or beer-houses. These, in this area which is richly served by reservoirs, would have been mostly in farmhouses and would have opened specially to cater for the hardworking and ever thirsty navvies who came from all over the country to build the dams. The village of Totley, on the far side of the city, was very similar when the Totley railway tunnel was being clawed and blasted out of the hillside.

There are four main reservoirs around the Bradfields. For my older readers, and for myself, I have used the tried and tested Imperial system when stating the various measurements:-

The Strines

This was completed in 1871. It has a surface area of 55 acres; its deepest part is estimated as being 67 feet and its total water capacity when full is 453 millions gallons.

The Dale Dyke

This was first completed in 1864, but following the bursting of the dam embankment in that year and the resulting huge loss of life and damage to property, it was redesigned and a new dam was constructed about 400 yards upstream. This reduced the holding capacity of the reservoir by about one third. It was finally finished in 1875. The original surface area was 78 acres, but this was reduced to 62 acres after the flood. Again, like The Strines, the deepest part is about 67 feet; its total water capacity when full is 466 million gallons.

The Agden

This was completed in 1869. It has a surface area of 63 acres; a deepest part of about 90 feet and a water capacity when full of 559 million gallons.

The Dam Flask

This is the largest of the four dams. Its surface area is 115 acres and its deepest part is 85 feet. It was completed in 1867, but wasn't fully utilised until 1896 due to design alterations. The total water capacity when full is a staggering 1,108 million gallons.

This is the most easily accessed of the dams and thus is the most popular stretch of water both for fishermen and sailors. In the beginning of the last century, the Sheffield Water Company reported proudly that they had "released 2,000 trout and a quantity of other large fish into the dam". Most of their descendents are probably still there, although I have never caught any, so can't swear to this!

The following two public houses were close to the church, for High Bradfield is an old village and both the church and the pubs were, in the olden days, focal points of village life.

The Cross Daggers, High Bradfield

This pub closed in about 1900 or possibly a handful of years earlier. The building then became the post office and when that closed, the building was converted into four flats.

Because of its close proximity to the gates of the church of St. Nicholas, it was initially known as "Heavens Parlour (or Parlur) and was part of the dwelling of one Jeremiah Parkin. It was at this time a beer-house. Historically, things at this time are a bit vague. It was once kept by a man described as a "clerk", perhaps a parish or church official. He was called Jerry, but it isn't known for certain whether this was the previously mentioned Mr Parkin or not. It could well have been. This Jerry, when on church business, especially on Sundays, or when there was a wedding or a funeral, always wore buckled shoes, black stockings, a tail coat and a wig. They had style in those days! This was in the 19th century, of course, but even today, especially among the judiciary, these things are still worn on ceremonial occasions, actually, I have a male friend....... I won't go on.

The pub became The Cross Daggers before 1833 when Ann Morton took over after Jerry's licence and she was followed by the well known local stone mason family, the Fox's. In 1895, a trade directory has Alfred Elliott as landlord. He also carried on a cutlery business with premises in West Bar, Sheffield. He was a knife blade forger. Shortly after that, The Crossed Daggers came to a sticky end when the licence was lost due to the violent behaviour of the navvies who frequented the pub and who at the time were in the district to work on the local reservoir dams.

The Old Horns, High Bradfield

The pub building, which stands today, was rebuilt c1830 by James Fox, probably on or near the site of an earlier public house of the same name. In 1833, the landlord was James Siddons, who was followed after 1841 by Henry Siddons, possibly his son. Charles Grayson had the pub from  1861 to 1864. William Cundy was there from 1865 until 1871 and then there was a landlady, Mrs Frances Woodhead. Up until 1893, there were two other landlords, Thomas Greaves and John Bashworth and then, in about 1895, Charles Fox took the licence. Mr Fox appears to have died or to have given up the pub following the death of his wife in 1903, because it was then that Charles Booth took the pub over. After Mr Booth, there were several changes - William and George Burnham, Colin Booth, possibly a relative of Charles Booth, and Wilton Morton. There have, of course, been a number of modern licensees.

The sign, The Old Horns, probably comes from the Bradfield Fair. The patron saint of the fair was St. Luke and this saint's symbol was the ox. There is an ox on a stained glass window in the church and also on the panelling of the pulpit. Because of this connection, a pair of horns played quite a large part in the ceremony of the day. The fair was held at Old Horns Yard and it often coincided with the annual Statute Hirings. This was a gathering when farmworkers and others came from all over the parish to be hired for a year. Contracts were sealed by the handing over of a "fastening" penny or by the slapping of hands.

The day of the fair was one of the busiest days of the year in High Bradfield and it was held on the last Friday in October. The village streets were packed out with stalls of all sorts and amusements such as an Aunt Sally and coconut shies. Other country entertainments, now against the law, but then extremely popular, were staged. These were cock-fighting, bull and bear baiting.

There cannot be much doubt that during the Fair days, a huge amount of eating and drinking went on. Why not? Farmworkers had little enough to ease the boredom and hardship of their lives. At the end of the 19th century, the Fair and the Statute Hirings began to die out and have since faded away completely.

Recently, The Old Horns was refurbished and is now one of the most popular of Sheffield's outlying county pubs. It is, I suppose, a pub restaurant now.

The stocks next to the Old Horns

A feature not connected to the pub, but a nice historic touch, are the **village stocks** which have been placed not far from the pub's front door. They are probably not the original and are not very old, but in days gone by there used to be a set in every village that had a church. It was common, when church attendance was compulsory, for non-attenders, who preferred the spiritual company inside the local pub, to be rooted out and locked in the stocks for a spell to reflect on the error of their ways!

Low Bradfield is not a village with a clearly defined centre. It is not so tightly knit as High Bradfield and covers a larger area. Although it cannot boast an old and attractive church like its neighbour, it has only ever had a chapel, now a house, it does have a very pleasant cricket ground where the great game has been played since at least 1890. This is skirted by the meandering Agden Beck which flows into the huge Dam Flask reservoir.

Beneath the cold waters of this reservoir lies the remains of The Barrel public house - I have seen this pub known as The Ball in old parish records. This pub was severely damaged and partially destroyed, as were a great many other buildings and businesses, during the Great Sheffield Flood, known here and often inscribed on tombstones, as the "Bradfield Inundation". This pub can be traced back to at least 1828, when it was mentioned in a licence application and would, I suppose, have been a beer-house. The landlord in 1833 was Benjamin Ibbotson. By 1841, the landlord was probably his son, John or Jonathan Ibbotson. He was still there at the time of the flood. I hope he was well insured!

I have heard about another beer-house called The Brooms in this area somewhere. It seems to have been a short lived place and would have been a farmhouse which opened purely and simply to supply beer to the navvies working on the reservoirs.

The Cross Inn, Woodfall Lane, Low Bradfield

This village centre pub was open for just over 100 years and was for most of this time a beer-house. It seems that it took its name from an ancient Celtic or Saxon granite cross which was dug up c1876 in one of the local fields. It is now by the wall of High Bradfield's St. Nicholas' Church, where it was placed in 1886.

The Drabble family were the first licensees. They were also clay merchants and would have dealt in both fireclay and the clay used in Sheffield to make the crucibles which were used in the steel making process invented by Benjamin Huntsman. Claymining was an important and profitable industry and in this area it was mostly centred around Ughill.

In 1865, which was probably when the pub first opened, Mark Drabble was recorded in a trade directory as being a beer retailer. He was followed by Hugh Drabble, perhaps his son, who was there until at least 1879. The pub was then taken over by Francis Wilson from c1890 until 1899, assisted by his wife, Ann. I don't know what the pub was called in the years before the cross was found - perhaps, like many beer-houses, it was just known by the name of the landlord.

In 1910, Mr Jepson and his family were running the pub; from c1930 until c1950, the pub was occupied by Fred Staniforth and his wife. When Mr Staniforth died in his early 50's, Stanley Hinds took over the licence. Mr Hinds was a nephew of Mrs Staniforth and, with his wife, he was licensee for about 25 years until 1975. This was when the pub's last landlord moved in and saw out the final three years of the pub's life.

Joe Murfin had the dubious honour of calling time and then closing the doors for good. He then left Low Bradfield to take over the running of The Farfield, Neepsend Lane, just beside Neepsend Bridge.

The reason that this nice little country pub, handy for the cricket ground in the summer, closed, can be blamed purely and simply because of a short-sighted attitude by the brewery which owned it. The toilets and drains of the building were old fashioned and needed upgrading to meet modern standards. The brewery refused to pay for these improvements, surely not a huge sum, and so the bureaucrats struck and the pub closed. It was, in my opinion and in the opinion of many others, a great loss to the village.

The Plough, New Road, Low Bradfield

Stone built and solid, this pub has the appearance of typical Yorkshire farm buildings, a tribute to the cruel winds which sometimes scour the village. It was first opened in the 1830's, when Benjamin Hobson was listed there as a victualler. Then, between c1841 and c1849, George Hollins was landlord. He was followed by George Woodhead who kept the pub from c1852 until c1865. This period includes the time of the "Bradfield Inundation" and it is said that the children of the village "fled to The Plough for safety"!

The following landlord had several jobs, as perhaps had his predecessors. This was not unusual in those days. As well as keeping the pub, Emmanuel Sanderson was also a wheelwright and carpenter. His sojourn at The Plough was from 1865 until 1876. Robert Bramall took over from him and he was also a man of several parts. He combined beer-house keeping with being a farmer and a butcher. When he departed, either just from the pub or from life altogether, Edward Smith took the licence. He died, aged only 54 years, at the pub in 1895 and he was followed by Francis Rider. Mr Rider was there until c1902, when George Hall became landlord.

The 20th century saw fewer landlords than the previous century. Henry Creswick was there for 12 years; Joseph Bramall spent many years behind the bar and the Huddleston's, Richard and Nellie, guided the pub into the 1970's.

During the Huddleston's reign, structural alterations aimed at enlarging the pub were carried out and it was during this upheaval that two pairs of well made childrens' boots were found hidden in the eaves. They were examined by experts and were thought to date from the 18th century. I wonder if this was some sort of a superstitious custom. I have heard of many things like this. In the West Country, and perhaps elsewhere, it used to be common to bury a coin, sometimes a sovereign, under either the front step or the hearthstone to bring good luck to the house. Also in East Anglia, especially Suffolk, cats have been found in the roofs and thatches of houses.

CHAPTER TEN
BRADFIELD DALE AND THE BRADFIELD HAMLETS

Bradfield Dale is widely spread and until very recently had two public houses. One is a seriously old former manor house and later coaching inn and the other was a former farm, which began life when part of the farm buildings were turned into a beer-house for navvies. It is now a private house, but still looks like the pub it was until the end of 1999.

The Strines, Mortimer Road, Bradfield Dale

This is one of the most isolated pubs which decorate the outer fringes of Sheffield. The buildings are old and attractive and were first built in either the 16th or 17th centuries - I favour the former - and was the family seat of the Worrall family. This family were at one time both important and prominent in the Bradfield area. This seems to be born out by the fact that a village nearby has the same name. Above the main entrance door to the pub, made out of the moorland granite, is the Worrall family coat of arms.

Two early members of the Worrall's, Anthony and Gervase, both left money for the betterment of the poor of Bradfield Parish. Their wills were dated 1761 and 1762 respectively and although the amount of money each left was only £10 per annum, in the 18th century this amount, now considered tiny, would have been worth far more. These were the days when a working man counted his wages in pennies, not in pounds! There are two Worrall men either buried or at least commemorated inside High Bradfield church.

There used to be, scratched on a window pane inside the pub, probably with a diamond, the following words, "Oh, Ye charming mistresse Dorothy Worrall". This lady was probably a daughter of the family and her suitor was John Kinge. They appear to have married, because in a 1562 marriage entry in the church register in High Bradfield is an entry, "John Kynge and Dorytye Worrall maryed the XXII day of February". The spelling of words was a more personal choice in those days. I wonder if we are heading back that way today?

The piece of glass has now gone and it is believed that it was removed by a member of the family and taken to London. Perhaps it is still a treasured possession somewhere.

For most of its long and lonely life, this pub has been known as The Strines (or sometimes Strynes). I have, in my researches in the Bradfield Council archives, aided by Malcolm Nunn, found an old licence application concerning this pub. In this old document, hand written in copperplate writing, it is called both The Tailors and The Taylors Arms. It is dated 1840.

The landlord in 1833 was John Earnshaw. A family recorded as landlords were the Elliotts. George was licensee between 1849 and 1865; John kept the pub in 1871 and his son, Charles, was there in 1881.

Charles Elliott was followed by the Horsfields, John and Jane. John Horsfield died in 1891, aged 88 years old, but his wife was still licensee in 1898.

Three 20th century landlords were George Cooper in 1904; David Thorpe between 1915 and 1922 and, in 1930, William Ayres. The pub building in use today is still mainly the old manor house, but as long ago as c1860, extension work was carried out.

As is common with very old buildings, not only public houses, legends appear. These may or may not be true and some, to be frank, are not terribly interesting, even taking into account the distortion and exaggeration which takes place over years of telling. Two such tales have attached themselves to The Strines; neither are particularly brilliant.

In either the 18th or 19th century, a tailor came to spend the night at the inn. He had been travelling round the district drumming up business. The story goes that prior to his arriving at the inn, he had been seen in possession of some ornaments, thought by their appearance to be made of gold. Where he had got them, no-one knew. After deciding to spend the night at the inn, he was never, ever, seen in the district again. The suspicion was widespread that the landlord of the inn knew more about his disappearance than he was prepared to admit. There is ample desolate moorland surrounding the inn in which to hide a body!

Regarding the tailor and his itinerant way of life. This was not at all uncommon in those days and even during the last century. Many tradesmen found it profitable to seek out business in this fashion.

"Herring Jack" sold a strange mixture of herrings and oranges, which he packed into a wicker basket and carried on his head. Johnny Robinson came weekly on his horse and cart which was loaded up with fruit and vegetables. "The Paraffin Man" announced his arrival by wielding a large brass handbell with gusto. He also toured the area on a horse and cart and, as well as selling paraffin, which was a much needed commodity in pre-electric days, from a large tank on the back of his cart, he also sold buckets, kettles, pots and pans and, most important, chamber pots!

Possibly the most well known of these traders was **"Stocking Johnny"**. He walked all the way from Honley, a small village between Holmfirth and Huddersfield. It was a fair trek to Bradfield and he carried his wares slung over his shoulder in two large, navy blue, triangular bags. His constant companions were his pipe and his umbrella. His range of goods was large, but light to carry. He sold black stockings made of cashmere, knickers, shoe laces, buttons, cotton and thread, needles and pins together with a range of patent medicines like Beecham's Pills and various cough mixtures. He also sold potions that he made up himself. He paid the local children to collect herbs for him. These, which included dandelions, yarrow and comfrey, he took home to use in his mixtures.

He was popular in the parish and had a selection of houses where he put up for the

night while doing his rounds of the villages. He
was a tall man, around six foot, and he always
dressed in black. He drank tea with no milk or
sugar, but with a raw egg cracked into it. It
sounds disgusting, but I suppose he needed
the energy it provided for the many miles
he had to walk.

The second tale about the inn, features
two daughters of the family, a serving
wench and the landlord himself. The
maid's lover was known by the two girls
to meet her at the back of the inn. So,
one night the two girls dressed up as men
and one went to the window to attract
the maid by whistling; the other girl hid
in the shadows. The landlord, hearing the
furtive whistle, went to the window and
blasted off with his shotgun at the shadowy
figure outside that he thought was a burglar.
The girl died of her wounds and the "joke"
ended in tragedy. It is said, of course, that at the
rear of the old inn is sometimes seen the ghostly figure
of a girl. Well, I never!

Stocking Johnny

There is also supposed to be a White Lady, who has allegedly been seen walking on
what used to be the drive that went up to the hall. There would be, wouldn't there?

The Haychatter, Bradfield Dale

This pub was part of a group of farm buildings which were known, as far back as
the early 17th century, as Haychatter Farm. This farm is first mentioned in a will of
1614 where it is referred to as Hechetter House. It was first recorded as a beer-house
in 1865.

During the construction work on the nearby dams, it made good business sense to
cash in on this short term boom if possible and turn a farm into a beer-house to
supply the navvies with the necessary beer that they needed after a hard day at the
reservoir. Many farms did this, but The Haychatter was one of the few which
remained a beer-house after the navvies had gone.

George Littlewood was the landlord between 1871 and 1881 and he was followed
by GH Shaw. Mr Shaw bought the farm and pub when it was sold by public
auction in 1880. The Crawshaw family, Fred and Elizabeth, ruled the roost in 1890
and they were followed by Henry Wilson from 1893. His wife, Mary Ann, died

there aged 64 in 1901 and Henry himself died there aged 77 in 1904.

After the Wilsons, Frederick Bramall was licensee until 1923 and Elias Uttley from 1923 until 1936. His wife carried on after his death until c1949. Then known as The Reservoir (I'm not sure when the name was changed, but it was a lot earlier than that), it was sold in 1949. It was described on the sales brochure as a licenced free-house with an attached farm and with a seven day beer licence.

The pub, together with the other buildings and some land, was bought by Mrs Florence Helliwell in November, 1962 and she sold it later to the Sheffield brewers, Tennant Brothers Ltd, for £15,000.

Mr and Mrs Siddall became licensees, but I am not certain when they took the pub over. I do know that Mr Siddall died in 1975 and his wife, Margaret, assumed the job of running the pub on her own. When I visited the pub in the spring of 1999, the Siddall name was still over the door, although it has since closed down.

The Haychatter was a secluded and hardly remembered pub, now with a full licence, on a narrow, damp and tree shrouded lane. It is well known among the locals of High Bradfield, for its rather eccentric opening hours. The name, Haychatter refers, I have been told, either to a noisy "chattering" machine which turned hay to ensure that it dried evenly, or to a whinchat, a small bird which lives in tall grass and hay and makes its nest from hay. I think that the pub sign favoured the bird.

A group of very old buildings such as these, especially if a pub is included somewhere, must have over the years garnered many tales and legends, but to my lasting regret, I can't find any.

The hamlets of Dungworth and Hill Top are slowly losing their isolated feel these days. Both are old settlements. The name of Hill Top seems to be self explanatory. Dungworth is slightly more difficult. The first historical mention of Dungworth occurred in the 13th century, in an old document of the period. But the meaning of the name? It doesn't sound too attractive! It could derive from, I've been told, a partially underground dwelling or simply a dwelling roofed with dung. This is not as unlikely as it sounds, as dung was used extensively in the middle ages as a building material, especially when building cottages by the wattle and daub method (the dung was the daub, the wattle was a network of thin saplings, often hazel). The things you can learn in a book about pubs!

The George, Hill Top

Closed down c1957, this pub dated from probably at least the early days of the 19th century. A landlord in those days was George Drabble, 1849. Fortunately, the buildings were preserved and now serve as a farmhouse.

As it was in most small villages and hamlets, the pub formed a centre for many of the local activities. There were a variety of teams based at the pub - cricket, football, skittles and also that venerable and now almost extinct Northern game, knur and spell, which I covered earlier in this book in some depth.

The pub, probably because of the rocky foundations upon which it was built, had no cellar and the barrels of beer were stored in a back room on the ground floor.

I believe that, like The Cross in Low Bradfield, the pub was forced to close because the brewery refused to spend money on upgrading the antiquated toilet facilities. I wonder if the brewery now regrets this short-sighted decision? After all, it is always easier to close a pub than open one!

The Royal Hotel, Dungworth

Built in c1850, the first landlord was Benjamin Ibbotson. He wasn't just a landlord, he was a coal merchant as well.

Again, in a similar manner to The George at nearby Hill Top, this pub would have played its part in the village activities, although as a larger place, Dungworth had other attractions. There was a Methodist chapel and a school together with a village hall, all of which were built in a fairly narrow time band in the

19th century. While these would have shared in hosting the village activities, the pub would still have had its place, after all, it was the only place which sold strong drink!

The pub is still in business and is a pleasant country free-house. The present licensees, David and Linda Lambert, always ensure that there is always a selection of real ales on tap and use, where possible, the small local breweries such as the Wentworth Brewery and the Kelham Island Brewery. They also provide good food and accommodation.

The Boot and Shoe, Dungworth

This short lived pub is described in early 19th century documents as being "on the road from Bradfield to Stannington". It seems that it was first opened, almost certainly as a beer-house, in 1834 when the landlord was John Wragg. He was described then as "a cordwainer and publican". Before I looked up this word, I had always thought that a cordwainer was something to do with ropemaking. It is in fact an old word for a shoemaker. You live and learn!

The possible site of this pub is now Yew Folds Farm.

It would be wrong to call Worrall a hamlet, even though, not having a parish church, it is technically that. It is too large and, with the increase in the number of new houses which are being built here, it seems that it will continue to grow.

The Shoulder of Mutton, Top Road, Worrall

This pub can be traced back to c1817 and is without doubt much older than that. It seems that originally it was built as a farmhouse. It is an impressive Yorkshire country building with thick stone walls, some leaded windows and oak beams.

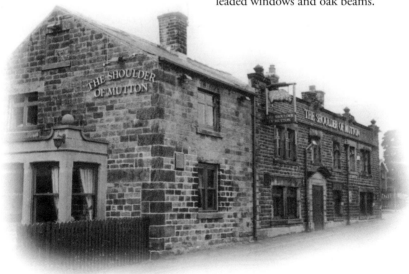

This is a very well known pub and although on maps before 1850, the position is merely given as "inn", as it was then a beer-house; on a map of 1895, the name is given. It is very frustrating that there is no more information available about this pub, but I think that it can be taken as read that the activities taking place years ago within its walls would have been similar to those happening at other pubs in the area. In 1825, the landlord was William Charlesworth and in 1833 and 1849, Joseph Charlesworth, who was probably son.

There is one tale connected with The Shoulder of Mutton which I feel is well worth telling. I read it in Mr Joe Castle's excellent book, "Roads to Worrall" and I have produced an abridged version of it here:-

A farmer from the Worrall area in the 1870's had a milk round in Hillsborough and each day, sometimes accompanied by his wife, probably if there was any heavy lifting to do, he travelled there with his milk float to serve his customers. It was his habit to sometimes withdraw money from a bank, while in Hillsborough, to pay for his usual household expenses.

One particular day, after finishing his round, he called into the bank, drew out a sum of money and he and his wife started back to Worrall. Arriving there, the farmer decided to call into The Shoulder of Mutton for a drink and so sent his wife on ahead with the milk float.

In the pub, drinking with people he was well acquainted with, he let slip to a neighbour that he'd been doing his milk round in Hillsborough and had drawn out quite a large sum of money from the bank - money that he still carried on his person. Walls, they say, have ears! And so do customers in public bars! Perhaps the farmer had, through drink, become a little too loud in his speech, but his conversation was overheard by another farmer who lived near to him. This man, so the story goes, badly needed money and saw this as an opportunity to get some.

He slipped quietly out of the pub and hid alongside the road that he knew the farmer would have to use to get home. When his victim passed, tipsy perhaps, but by no means drunk, he leapt out of the hedge and beat him savagely about the head with a billet of wood.

The farmer was taken completely by surprise and was soon overcome and badly injured. His assailant ransacked his pockets, stole all the money that he could find and made off home leaving the farmer lying at the side of the road. There he died, so serious were his injuries.

His attacker, upon arriving home with his clothes heavily bloodstained, was naturally questioned by his wife, but he swore her to secrecy about his crime.

However, due perhaps to the fact that he was known to be in need of money, or perhaps because he had been seen leaving the pub early, he was arrested and tried for the murder of the farmer. He was acquitted through lack of evidence or witnesses. In those days forensic science was unknown.

It wasn't long before he and his family left the district. Perhaps he had been tried and found guilty by his peers and could no longer stand the whispers and accusing fingers which, since the murder, had dogged his footsteps!

The Blue Ball, Haggstones Road, Worrall

I believe that many years ago there used to be a pub called The Ball in Haggstones Road. There is no trace of it today - did it become the present Blue Ball? I think that this is possible.

It seems that the present pub began life as a pair of workers cottages with outbuildings beside them. These cottages, much altered, make up the pub buildings today, but the outbuildings, which lasted until c1970, have disappeared beneath the carpark.

The Blue Ball was one of the meeting places of the Ecclesfield Beagles. This hunt was not, as is more normal in the Midlands and South of England, concerned with hunting foxes. The prey here were hares. Most of the hunt followers would have been on foot, although the hunt servants and a few of the wealthier supporters would have been mounted.

Another regular stop outside the pub was the horse-drawn bus to The Greyhound pub in Gibraltar Street, Sheffield. This was the once a day public transport to and from Sheffield - miss it and you walked!

Early landlords included:- Robert Waite, 1825; Thomas Turner, c1833 until c1851, who was also a quarry owner - this could have been either a stone or gannister quarry. He was followed by Joseph Senior, 1852; Joseph Woolhouse, c1852 until c1862 and John Grayson from 1884 until at least 1898.

The Brown Cow, Top Road, Worrall

Now closed and a private house, its building was almost opposite The Shoulder of Mutton.

Wharncliffe Side straggles along the main road to Manchester. It has begun to spread out now as new housing is built, but it is surprising that this small settlement has had, and still has, so many pubs. It probably dates from the days when this was a turnpike road. It seems likely that the Earls of Wharncliffe, who were created from the local Wortley family in 1876, took their title from this hamlet.

The Blue Ball, Main Road, Wharncliffe Side

In common with the pub of the same name in Worrall, and in other parts of both Sheffield and England, pubs with this name took it from the crystal ball of the fortune-teller. It is not unusual today to have pub signs with some sort of sporting theme involving a ball, usually something really crass like snooker, but this is incorrect.

This pub is still open and was there in 1833, when the landlord was John Morton. He was followed by Joseph Senior, 1849.

The Wharncliffe Arms, Main Road, Wharncliffe Side

This pub is still open. It is an attractive old building, a couple of hundred yards nearer to Sheffield than The Blue Ball, but I know little about its history. It, like the akjacent Blue Ball, has all the hallmarks of an old turnpike pub.

The Traveller's Inn (or Arms), Wharncliffe Side

There is a pub mentioned historically with this name. I know a little about it, but I've little idea of where it used to be. In the 1840's it was kept by the Lingard Family - Ann, Robert and Caleb. It was still there in 1856. I believe that a building beside The Wharncliffe Arms used to be a pub. Is it possible that this was the site of The Traveller's Inn?

The final group of pubs are in Midhopestones and the beautifully named Wigtwizzle. Unfortunately, of these three pubs, none are still open.

The Midhopestones Arms, Midhopestones

This was formerly known as The Club and then, in 1840, The Barrel. Between 1841 and 1849, Joseph Kay was the landlord.

This pub closed for business on 16 October, 1999 after serving the village of Midhopestones for many years. The reason given was one which has closed so many village pubs - it wasn't making enough money to stay open and pay its bills.

The closure caused a good deal of upset and it was for the usual, short-sighted and selfish reason which goes something like this - the villagers have always had a pub; they consider it to be "their" pub and even if they hardly, if at all, use it, they consider that it should remain open as it is "part of the village"! It matters not that the (in this case) landlady, was losing money hand over fist and often hardly sold a drink all night.

When she recently tried to obtain planning permission to turn the pub building into three cottages, a very reaasonable application I would have thought, permission was refused. So, what happens now? She can hardly be forced to reopen the pub and run it at a loss, can she? Sometimes I despair, I really do!

The Rose and Crown, Midhopestones

This pub has been closed for a number of years and I know nothing about its history.

The Sportsman's Arms, Wigtwizzle

In 1841, the landlord was Thomas Hollins; in 1849, Henry Hollins, possibly his son. The date when this pub was demolished is not known. In old documents, I have seen the name Wigtwizzle spelt as Wightwizzle.

CHAPTER ELEVEN
STANNINGTON

Part of the village of Stannington lies in the Parish of Bradfield. Here is the highest part of Sheffield; every road seems to be climbing uphill. It is a well spaced out, well populated and increasingly newly built village. It's a popular place to leave in the morning to go to work elsewhere. One of the reasons for this is its lack of industrial opportunities today, although in the past it was rooted in the cutlery trades.

One famous son, who is now long dead, was the great-grandfather of George Wostenholm, one of Sheffield's legendry cutlery "barons". Also known as George, he set himself up as a cutler in Stannington in 1745. He was followed by his son, Henry, who was shortly followed in his turn by his son, George. The tradition was well set up.

In 1776, George moved his expanding business to Sheffield. First to Garden Street and then to larger premises in Broad Lane. The final move was to Rockingham Street. This was to take over a workshop beside the site upon which the Wostenholm's purpose built cutlery factory was built in 1815.

The third George Wostenholm, and the one best remembered, was then 15 years old and already well into learning the craft of cutler. When he died, aged 76 years old, he left a reputation not only as a hard and exacting man to work for, but also for the quality of the products his factory produced.

So dedicated was George to getting things right, that he changed the family name from Wolstenholme to Wostenholm so that it would fit more easily onto his knife blades. Now that is dedication!

Stannington has a fine collection of pubs, both old and new.

The Anvil, Stannington Road

I suppose that strictly speaking, this pub is not quite in Stannington, being as it is on the road leading to the village. It is logical to suppose that it took its name from the nearby Mousehole Forge which, apart from making various types of hardware, specialised in making award winning anvils. They produced a wide range of different types of these important engineering tools, as many as 12 assorted sorts and shapes. This forge, situated slightly down the hill from the pub and on the opposite side of the road near to the River Rivelin, would have used the river for its main and all important source of water both for driving and cooling purposes.

The Anvil is mentioned in a trade directory of 1825 when the landlord was George Thompson. He was followed by Samuel Marples, 1833; Sarah Marples, 1841 and Alfred Nuttall, 1849. A modern landlord was Ted Catlin, a former captain of Sheffield Wednesday FC.

It appears that there used to be an earlier version of this pub on an adjoining site.

The Sportsman, Oldfield Road

The original pub which stood near to this spot was formally a farmhouse and has long since been demolished and the present building stands on the very edge of Stannington village. Early landlords were John Inman (another one!), 1833; Joshua Mallinson, 1849 and up to March, 1852, Stephen Farmery - he was also a farmer. He

was followed by a cutler named Luke Furness. Various members of the Gray family were, for more than 50 years, the licencees. They also were connected to the Hare and Hounds and indeed a local name for Uppergate is "Grays Hill".

The Crown & Glove, Uppergate Road

The Top House

This pub, according to old property deed, was once a beer-house and was part of a terrace of four cottages. It was owned by a syndicate of several people and was known as The Tontine. This word means, according to the Oxford Dictionary, "a financial arrangement by which the benefits of the surviving participants are increased on the death or default of any one of them". This sounds a bit technical for Sheffield, but there was a large and famous coaching inn of that name, which used at one time to stand in The Haymarket in Sheffield. It was demolished by the Duke of Norfolk to build his market halls. From about 1842 the name was changed to the Crown and Glove

I doubt whether many people have heard of the Dymoke family. For a great number of years, this family held the ancient heraldic title of King's (or Queen's) Champion. This may have involved many duties in the middle ages, but for the last hundred years or so, all it meant was that before the sovereign was crowned, the champion cast down a glove on to the ground. Anyone who picked up the glove indicated that they objected to the coronation taking place and thus had to fight the champion in combat. I don't know if this title is still relevant today, but it is a nice piece of old English history. This, then, is how the Crown and Glove got it's name. Known to locals as the "Top House" it is supposed to be perched on one of Sheffield's seven hills and to be the

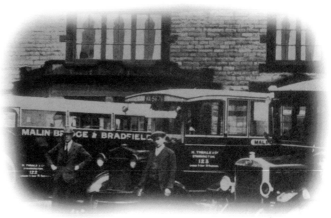

Mr Thrales and his bus company

highest pub in the area. It is also supposed to be on the highest point between England and the Ural mountains in what used to be the USSR.

One of the early 20th century landlords, Mr H Thrales, ran both the pub and a three unit bus service from the pub carpark to Malin Bridge. From there they trundled along Loxley Road to High Bradfield, down to Low Bradfield and back around Dam Flask to Malin Bridge and then to Stannington. It seems a nice piece of enterprise and I would think that it did very well. This was around the middle of the 1920's.

Some earlier landlords were:- Charles Cheek, 1825; Joseph Gosney, 1833; William Revitt, 1841; Hugh Ibbotson, 1849; Thomas Oates, who was also by trade a needle grinder and William Franklin. None of these men seems to have held the licence for very long.

Today, this popular pub caters for several tastes. In what must be called the "public bar", the old games of cribbage and dominos are still popular, rather than the noisy modern additions of juke box, television and video games. The pub contains a large and interesting collection of old brasses and many photographs and paintings line just about every piece of wall.

The Rose and Crown, Bankfield Lane

The information available about this pub is sparse, but it seems that it began as a private house and then, probably, sometime in the 19th century, it became a beer-house. In the years up to 1918, when it was sold to Henry Tomlinson's Brewery, Anchor Brewery, Cherry Street, it had for a long time been owned by members of the Wild family.

In 1920, Irvine Lee and his wife, Minnie, became the tenants. It was a long stay and, after Mr Lee passed away in 1953, his wife took over and was there for many years. She was a popular licensee and the nickname of "Minnies" for the pub is still recognised in Stannington.

So great was the understanding that she built up with her regular customers that her habit of leaving her change in a jar on a table unattended was respected by all and there was never any suggestion of anyone interfering with it. Not many places can say that today!

The smallish, detached building is a popular and attractive pub which stands just a little away from the hustle and bustle of the village.

The Peacock, Stannington Road, Knowle Top

This former farmhouse has been a pub since at least 1825, when the landlord was Joseph Marples. He was followed by George Tompson and then, up to 7th April 1846 John Marsh (or March) was licensee. He was also a working blacksmith and his smithy and forge used to stand next to the pub buildings. When he either retired or died, the licence was transferred to his son, George. He had learned his father's trade and he also did some small scale farming.

The Peacock was mentioned in the now defunct newspaper, The Sheffield Weekly News on 9th August 1919, in an article describing an event which happened on 16th October, 1828. This was the day that the foundation stone of Stannington Church was laid. Following the ceremony, the "quality" all retired to The Peacock for tea whilst the village children and villagers sang outside. People knew their place in those days!

A story is told about a disgruntled customer who, after being barred by a 19th century landlord, took his revenge by cutting the legs of the man's trousers as they were hung out to dry on the pub washing line. It is believed that he then said, "That will bring him down to my level!" No way really to get back into the landlord's favour, but probably very satisfying.

Two long serving landlords after the Second World War were Jack Mayos, who held the licence for about 20 years and before him an even longer serving licensee, Willis Bradshaw, was there for about 25 years. Now owned by Tom Cobleigh Ltd. this pub has a fine collection of colourful hanging baskets outside in the summer and is another country pub which makes a large part of its income from its restaurant trade.

There are numerous people who don't like the way that large pub companies take over country pubs and modernise them, spending huge sums of money in the process, and thus alter the entire ambience of the place. There is, of course, an alternative. The pub could close. About seven country pubs a week are already doing that!

The Queen's Hotel, Nook Lane/Stannington Road

This pub closed for business in 1913 when John Milner held the licence. The building is still there and is a private house. For over 30 years, after it closed as a pub, up until c1960, it did duty as the local police station. The entrance was on the side of the building and has now been bricked up, but the police sign can still be seen if you look very carefully.

It first opened as a pub in 1840, when George Dyson, who was also a pocket knife scale presser, applied for a licence to retail beer on the premises. In 1851, Matthew Oates, who was also a pocket knife blade forger, was in charge. It was once known as The Cricketers.

There was a short lived pub called The Park Head Tavern. On 17th December, 1842, according to Bradfield Council archives, the licence of this pub was transferred from Robert Furniss to William Fox. In the 1851 census, Mr Fox was described as a 51 year old razor scale presser, but in 1849, William Grayson was recorded as landlord. Not much else is known about this pub, even it's location has been lost in time.

Mentioned in licencing documents of the 19th century, in Bradfield Council archives, there is a mention of a Crawshaw Head Inn. This was situated somewhere just past Crawshaw Lodge on the road outside Stannington known as Rod Side. Nothing much else is known about it, although I suppose that as the area is mostly uninhabited and surrounded by rough moorland, any public house here would have been a small, wayside beer-house for travellers. A regular clientele there isn't!

The Deerstalker Inn, Deer Park Road

This is another pub of similar age and ambience as The Charles Turnbull. It probably got its name from the road it stands on. This got its name from the deer that used to roam the area many years ago. After all, a deerstalker would be at home in a deer park.

The Charles Turnbull, Liberty Hill

This is a modern, appallingly designed, "estate" type pub situated on the fringe of the village. It was, for some reason, named after a director of the parent brewery, Tetleys. It has little merit or atmosphere.

The Hare and Hounds, Church Street

The original Hare and Hounds was in Uppergate Road, (Grays Hill). In c1962 the incumbent landlord Sid Gray fell asleep with a lit pipe on his person and set himself on fire, he crawled into the pub yard and, unfortunately, later died from his burns. The old pub, itself, was never set on fire, as some people have mistakenly stated.

The present Hare and Hounds was built on Church Street in the mid to late 60s.

The old pub had several names. At the end of the 18th century it is recorded as being called The Well Green House, but whether it was a pub then I don't know; it was later called The Blue Boar and only became The Hare and Hounds in c1837. It was a free-house until it was bought in 1900 by John Smith's Brewery from Tadcaster. It is now a free house.

Between c1841 and c1849, the landlord was John Inman. Inman also doubled up as a shoemaker.

The present day independently run public house has a pleasant welcoming feel and is a focal point in the village of Stannington with its regular guest beers and home cooked Sunday lunches, barbecues, bungee jumps, quiz nights, car boot sales and various other events that Tim Broadhead and Penny Abbott regularly put on offer.

It is a meeting place for the British Legion, Stannington Hares football team and Stannington Chess club

CHAPTER TWELVE
WADSLEY VILLAGE

Like many villages which used to form the perimeter of Sheffield, Wadsley was probably first settled as far back as the Bronze Age or even earlier. It was never a large village and by the 19th century it had settled down into a collection of old granite cottages with a church, some almshouses, a school, and some public houses. This was roughly how the centre of the village was; around it were scattered various farms and other outlying buildings.

The main occupation in those days, apart from agriculture, seems to have been pen or pocket knife making with the odd brush maker thrown in.

The reputation of the cutlery workers of Wadsley Village does not appear to have been very high among their peers in other parts of Sheffield. It was said that when a Wadsley Village knife maker took his sack of knives into Sheffield to sell them, he had to be careful not to knock the sack, in case the rivets fell out of the handles! Not true, I'm sure.

There have been several buildings in the village which can honestly be described as "fine". Among them Loxley House, today a Grade II listed building, which was built in 1795 and improved in 1826; Owlerton Hall, now demolished; Dykes Hall, rebuilt by Sir John Fowler in 1852 but now also gone.

The pick of this crop though is Wadsley Hall. This is also Grade II listed and is a grand old building which stands on even older foundations. The hall which exists today is the one built by the then Lord of the Manor, George Bamforth in 1722. Previous to that, there was a hall which was owned in turn by a variety of people.

In 1547, just about the earliest date known, it was the property of a yeoman farmer called Griff. In 1557, it was the home of the Swyft family and a few years later, in 1590, it was owned by the seventh Earl of Shrewsbury, then by the eighth Earl, after which it passed, by marriage, to the Dukes of Norfolk.

Occupiers of the "new" hall included the Creswick family, who produced one of the best landscape painters that Sheffield has ever had - Thomas Creswick RA. He was born at the hall, as was another of Sheffield's unsung heroes, Sir John Fowler, 1817-1898. Sir John, whose name is practically unknown in the city today, had a hand in designing and building Wicker Arches. He then designed the Firth Railway Bridge and large parts of the London underground system. For these engineering feats, he received a Baronetcy from Queen Victoria. This is now extinct.

A later member of the Fowler family, Sir John Edward Fowler, was killed in the First World War, but before his death he gave free use of the hall to some of the many Belgian refugees, who flooded into England when the war made their position in their own country untenable.

I have elongated my coverage of Wadsley Village to include the Park Hotel, Wadsley Lane, but I haven't crossed the River Don to include Wadsley Bridge, because this clutch of four pubs was mentioned in my previous book *(A Pub On Every Corner)*.

I will mention Leppings Lane though, but only because of the old stepping stones and the bridges. The lane got its name from the "leaping" stones which crossed the river roughly where the modern Wadsley Bridge stands today; carts and horses were able to ford the river and the stones were used by the pedestrians. Then, probably in the 17th century, a wooden bridge was built and this was replaced by a stone bridge in 1777.

The Wadsley Jack, Rural Lane

This pub was formerly called The Star Inn, but sometime this century it took the name of a local mythical person, Wadsley Jack. This man was the creation of a 19th century local writer, Rueben Hallam, 1818-1908, at the instigation of the owner of the Sheffield Telegraph, Sir William Leng.

The idea was to publish a story every week which included various villages and thus when people bought the newspaper to read about their village, or to see if it was included in the story, the circulation of the newspaper would increase. It seemed to work, because Wadsley Jack became a hugely popular character.

Jack was described as an itinerant scissor grinder, who toured the Sheffield area and his supposed adventures were recorded by Mr Hallam, who was himself a local "character". He sported a huge and bushy white beard, was at one time the landlord of a pub, and lived to be ninety.

This old pub is made up of a fine and cosy collection of small rooms and is one of the few Sheffield pubs which still supports an actively used bowling green. It is an interesting building. Outside, beside the

pub, stands a set of stocks. These, or at least the stock stones, could be the old village stocks. Strangely enough, while the stocks are Grade II listed, the pub buildings aren't.

A landlady from early in the 19th century was Mary Baker, 1825 and 1833. She was followed by Thomas Knott, 1841 and 1852, who was also a cabinet maker by trade - and had a name to suit.

The Rose and Crown, Stour Lane

This pub was built c1848, when the first landlord was George Rose, another fitting name. A later landlord was William Marsh.

I have been told that in its early days the pub, probably a beer-house, was open all hours day and night.

As in the early 19th century, there were virtually no licencing restrictions, I don't see why not, especially if the landlord could make it pay and also stand the pace!

In the 1960's, the owners, Tetley's Brewery, bought the adjoining cottages to the rear of the pub, knocked through and extended the pub. This has resulted in different floor levels between rooms.

It used to be referred to as "The Jungle" or "The Top House". It is now a Grade II listed building.

The Sportsman, Worrall Road

Information about this pub is sparse. I know that it is old and that the landlord in 1841 was George Hoyle followed by Samuel Colley in 1849 and 1852.

It is a large, detached granite building, at the top of the hill, almost opposite the church. Former farmhouse perhaps?

The Horse and Jockey, Wadsley Lane

A very old pub which stands back slightly from the road, it is opposite where Wadsley Green used to be. This is where the local fairs were held. These old local gatherings, now extinct, could have dated back as far as the very early 14th century. This was when King Edward I granted the then Lord of the Manor, Robert de Wadsley, a Friday market day and an annual three day fair.

It was the custom at one time for the landlord of the pub to present copper kettles as prizes for events held at the fair. This led to the pub being nicknamed "The Copper Kettle", but it was never its official name. The pub has been, however, called The Bay Horse. The present building was erected in the 1930's. It is in the pseudo Tudor-style which was common at that period. Inside it is the standard "olde worlde" look produced by the brewery designers.

In 1833, the landlord was John Green, then Ruth Green, his widow, in 1841 and 1849. She was followed by Joseph Colley in 1852.

I once knew a landlord of this pub about 20 years ago, whose daily intake of Whitbread Gold Label Barley Wine was legendary. He's dead now.

The former Rock Inn

The Rock Inn (or House), Stour Lane

Now a private house, it stands beside The Rose and Crown. It opened in 1871 as a beer-house and when it closed sixty years later, it was still a beer-house. This is unusual as most pubs upgraded their licence at the earliest opportunity.

The first licence holder was Margaret Foxton, whose had previously run the adjacent Rose and Crown.

The Castle, Dykes Hall Road / Findon Street

This old pub is the corner building of a terrace of granite built houses. I know little about it, apart from the fact that it has hardly been touched by the usual "improvements" which have ruined so many public houses during the last few years. It can best be described as a surviving corner pub with several self-contained rooms and a central bar.

The Park Hotel, Wadsley Lane

This Edwardian pub, built in 1907, may perhaps be on the site of a previous pub, but I have no proof of this. There used to be a bowling green beside the pub, but as usual it is now a carpark. In 1966, when World Cup matches were played at the Sheffield Wednesday ground, German footballers were accommodated at the hotel. Today, it has two large and well appointed bars and advertises an upstairs function room for hire. It has all the makings of an ideal pub; it probably is an ideal pub. Why then does it depress me? Is it because it seems to me to completely lack atmosphere? Perhaps so.

The Beehive, Dykes Hall Road/Far Lane

The original pub of this name stood on the opposite side of the road junction. It was then a typical corner pub and was part of a terrace of houses. It was demolished in the late 1920's, probably for the usual road widening and a new, large, detached pub was built on the opposite corner. It is in the mock Tudor-style, similar, but larger than The Horse and Jockey. It looks out of place and would probably fit in better in the centre of a large housing estate.

CHAPTER THIRTEEN
OUGHTIBRIDGE

Another busy village is Oughtibridge. It squats beside the River Don and, in spite of its country surroundings, is cursed by the heavy traffic which uses the main road as it carves its way through the village. This road forms the conduit along which rush the heavy lorries, the light lorries and the cars on their way to Huddersfield, Manchester or the MI motorway. There is little remaining now of what once was a peaceful, rural community. The village is also bedevilled by a one-way system designed in Hell.

Here, the motor vehicle rules with a steel and noisy hand. There is, however, a thick vein of public houses in the village. A surprising amount for a place of this size - nine in all. Six of them are still alive; three are long dead.

Back along Middlewood Road towards Hillsborough is what remains of Middlewood Hospital. Opened in 1872, this grim place was initially known as The South Yorkshire Asylum and it has always maintained an uneasy relationship with Sheffield. In the past, many children, as a last resort, were threatened with the fate of "ending up in Middlewood" to keep them in order, so from a young age Sheffielders learned to fear the threatening, dark stone walls of the hospital.

It was designed by Bernard Hartley and is a typical, seriously ornate Victorian set of institutional buildings. Here there was little allowed by way of levity in the architecture. It was designed as a mental hospital and it looked the part! I have read that it was, in fact, not that bad and that it had large and airy ward blocks set in well kept and spacious gardens. So it is said!

During the First World War, the hospital became known as The Wharncliffe War Hospital and it was given over, to a large extent, to the treatment of the many men who had been disabled by the poisonous gas which was criminally used by both sides during the war.

After the war ended, and the last of the patients had either died or been moved somewhere else, the name was changed to The Middlewood Hospital and it resumed its role of treating the mentally ill.

Today, following the customary several years of dereliction, which every empty site has to suffer in Sheffield before anything is done to improve the situation, most of the satellite buildings have been demolished and a development of several hundred houses is under way; much of the once carefully manicured gardens will provide space for these. So, all that is really left of the old horror is the main Victorian block and the church.

There were two evils possible when the hospital closed down - one was to clear the site and allow it to revert to a green and pleasant park around the church with perhaps a small memorial or two to remind strollers of the history of the place; the other was to turn it into yet another upmarket complex of small houses. I don't know which was the lesser of these two evils or whether the best one was chosen.

The Station Inn, Station Lane

This former Tetley's pub was once to be found down a small lane which branched off what is called locally Jaw Bone Hill, but which is correctly named on road maps as Whale Jaw Hill.

As its name suggests, the inn was very close to the railway and has been converted into three private cottages, part of a terrace of the same, since it closed for the last time in 1963. Oughtibridge Station was in use when the electrified line from Sheffield to Manchester via the Woodhead Tunnel was

operating. The pub, which used to be owned by Duncan Gilmour's before Tetley's's took them over, closed some time before the railway.

The station first opened in 1845, so perhaps this gives some indication of the date when the pub opened. After closure, the station buildings were used by various enterprises, the last of these being Yorkshire Tarmac from c1982 until recently. When I visited the site in 1999, it was slowly falling to pieces, which is a shame as it would make a grand house for anyone with a few grand to spare.

The last landlord and landlady of the pub were Charlie and Doreen Mieszckak. They took it over in 1961 and, then at the age of 18, Doreen must have been one of the youngest landladies in the country. She is a very nice lady who now lives in Wharncliffe Side.

The Traveller's Rest, Langsett Road South

This narrow and strangely designed, two and three storey pub faces onto the main road through the village in both directions, both front and back, as it stands on a narrow spit of land. It is one of the few Samuel Smith pubs in the Sheffield area. Their beer is, I believe, an acquired taste.

The Middlewood Tavern, Middlewood Road

This popular and sometimes a trifle boisterous pub is beside the main road, near to the River Don, which flows past in its valley on the opposite side of the road. It is probably a little too far outside Oughtibridge to be claimed as one of this villages pubs and is, in fact, adjacent to the former Middlewood Hospital.

The tavern was open in 1839, possibly earlier, when the landlord was Joseph Hague; in 1841 it was

Early Charabanc or Wagonette

Samuel Wood and in 1856, the licence was passed, according to papers lodged in Bradfield Council archives, from William Bailey to John Bailey, who was probably his son.

The Stanley Arms, Langsett Road South / Church Street

This pub was demolished in c1960, as was much of the centre of the village to make way for modern housing. This was possibly the oldest pub in the village. On the site is now a complex of elderly persons flats, Westnall House.

The earliest landlord that I can find was Martin Stanley, 1825 - hence perhaps the pub's name. He was still there in 1841; in 1849, the landlord was Jonathan Rhodes and in 1852, George Woolhouse.

The Hare and Hounds, Church Street

This typical solid, granite built pub, with its popular country name is still open and must have been for many years, although I have been able to find out nothing about its history.

It is part of a short terrace of houses sloping down the hill and was very likely used as one or two cottages before it became a pub.

The Filesmith's Arms, Langsett Road South

Now closed since c1914, the building has been a village shop for many years with a chip shop and a newsagents as neighbours. This is very much a Sheffield trade name for a pub and there have been at least half a dozen more so named pubs, all in Sheffield city area. In 1843, the landlord was Thomas Garside, then in 1849 and 1852, John Holdsworth.

The White Hart, Langsett Road North

Open in 1825, when the landlord was Thomas Brammall. He remained in the pub until at least 1849. In 1852, the landlord was Thomas Turner. An early 20th century landlady was Mrs Ann Brammall, 1905. She appears as the landlady of The Castle Inn, Bolsterstone in 1907.

The White Hart

c100 years ago

c40 years ago

The Pheasant, Station Lane

There in 1825, but I have been able to find out little about its history. The detached building sits at the bottom of the road down the hill from Grenoside where Wale Jaw Hill merges with Station Lane. The surrounding area is slowly disappearing beneath an encroaching tide of new housing.

The Cock Inn, Bridge Hill

The landlord of this nice pub was John Fairest in 1833; in 1835, John Burkinshaw; in 1849, Willoughby Howe; in 1840, William Fairest and in 1905, another John Fairest. He was also a stone mason. I wonder if he was related to the John Fairest Ltd who run a very successful undertakers in Wadsley Bridge? This is another attractive, granite built pub which shares its site with what seems to have once been some sort of commercial building. The bar meals and decor are very good.

CHAPTER FOURTEEN
THE RIVELIN AND LOXLEY VALLEYS

If you travel along Loxley Road towards Dam Flask and the Bradfields, on the left is the meandering path of the River Loxley. Coyly hidden beneath its sheltering trees, this small river, quiet now, was once ant-busy, its banks clear of undergrowth and hindering vegetation. Waterpower was sought here and the grinding hulls and wheels huddled close to the river source. There were, in the 18th and 19th centuries, at least eight mill dams, several weirs and many water wheels. These wheels would often power different types of machinery during their lives - tilt hammers, grinding wheels, rolling mills for steel, wire, cloth and glass mills, mills for crushing clay or grinding corn. Water, the motive force, was indispensable.

One of the last water wheels (photo 1999)

It was, along the length of the river, an area of bustling activity which gave employment to a large number of the men from the area and also from further afield - it wasn't unusual, in those days, to walk 10 miles to work and back

Today, the river wanders quietly down the valley to join the Rivelin and then the Don, its flow strangled by the needs of the huge Dam Flask reservoir further up the valley. The few buildings that are left are now ruined heaps of masonry. A couple of the dams are kept clear for anglers and the wildlife has taken the river valley back. Both this place and the valley of the River Rivelin are fine places to walk through and explore.

The three pubs that are beside Loxley Road are all still open:-

The Admiral Rodney

This public house is marked on a map of 1890 as an unnamed smithy and inn and was probably, at that time, a beer- or ale-house. It was named after George Rodney, a British Admiral. He served with distinction in both the Seven Years War, 1756-1763, and the American War of Independence, 1775-1781. He was born in 1719, created Baron Rodney in 1782 and died in 1792. Today, the title is still in existence and there is a 10th Baron Rodney.

Formerly known as The Bold Rodney, the original pub can be traced back at least to 1833 through trade directories, although it seems likely that the pub was in business earlier than that date. Perhaps it was open at the time of the "Bold Admiral's" triumphs.

The present building, at the junction of Loxley Road with Rodney Lane, was built in c1957. Before that, the original pub building had beside it a blacksmiths forge and smithy and a large granite water trough - in those days a prudent man looked after his horses, for there was little else to use for mobile power or transport. These buildings, along with the pub building, went when the new public house was built. The forge site is now the pub carpark.

Some early landlords included Thomas Wilde, 1833, and William Fearn, 1849. Mr Fearn, unsurprisingly, was also by trade a blacksmith.

The Wisewood Inn

Like The Admiral Rodney, this pub is marked on a map of 1890 as an unnamed inn. Over 150 years old, this compact pub is the nearest of the three on Loxley Road to Malin Bridge. The landlord in 1841 was Benjamin Trickett and in 1849, William Wordsworth (another one!) There used to be a legendary landlady who also kept The Admiral Rodney for many years.

The Nag's Head Inn

On a map of 1901, this pub is shown by name which meant that it was fully licenced and could retail the full range of strong drink. It is an isolated pub, but pleasant and popular, although rather a "clique" seem, to use it.

The pub's name, The Nag's Head, has always been popular in this country. It refers, of course, to a horse, usually a saddle horse.

The Bridge Inn, Rowell Lane

There used to be a nearby fourth pub, but not on Loxley Road. This was down Rowell Lane, which leads off the road and is a way to Stannington. Not far down this lane, beside a bridge, there used to be a mill dam, now silted up. The pub, probably a beer-house, was nicknamed The Muck 'Oyle, This seems to give a fairly clear picture of what it was like!

The buildings were part beer-house and part flour mill. In 1838-1849, Jonathan Revitt, and in 1864, John Waters, are recorded as being both millers and victuallers.

The buildings were severely damaged in 1864 during the Great Flood, when further up the Loxley Valley, the new dam at Dale Dyke burst open sending well over a million tons of water roaring down the valley, through

Malin Bridge and Hillsborough and on towards Sheffield. It was an historic tragedy, still discussed in the area's local history groups. About 240 people were killed that dreadful night - either drowned or battered to death by the force of the flood water; many forges and waterwheels were destroyed and a huge number of houses were either washed away or badly damaged.

The pub and the mill probably never recovered from that March night, but today some of the buildings are still standing and are called Croft House.

There is one other pub within a stones throw of the Loxley Valley:-

The Robin Hood, Greaves Lane, Little Matlock

This pub was built in 1804 by the Rev. Thomas Halliday and from the outside it is not difficult to equate its appearance with that of a chapel. It is a large, four square millstone grit building, grim and uncompromising - out of place in these intensely rural surroundings. I have, on occasion, read that this pub was once known as The Robin Hood and Little John, but true or not, Little John has been abandoned.

After the pub was built, the area bordering it was landscaped and planted with trees and shrubs to attract the "gentry" of Sheffield to the woodland walks and scenes. It is now a wilderness, but faint traces of mans interference with nature can still be seen. The location, Little Matlock, takes its name from the Derbyshire village of Matlock which it is said to resemble. It is also reputed to be the birthplace of Robin Hood (another one!).

In 1833 and 1841, the landlord was John Rushey; in 1849, John Rushforth and in 1857, James Wragg. A family named Furness had connections to this pub from 1866 until the last of them, Matthew, retired from the trade in 1952.

Today, across from the car park, there is a small menagerie with a pony, cage birds and small animals, which is aimed at attracting couples with children. During the Second World War, old mine workings beneath the pub were used as an air raid shelter.

The River Rivelin has carved itself a deep and wandering valley between the convergence of the river with the River Loxley at Malin Bridge and Rivelin Post Office about two miles away towards Manchester. Once this was, like the Loxley Valley, a hive of industry from at least the 16th century. Mills to grind flour were the first to utilise the free water power available here, but these were soon followed, as the metal trades developed, by forges and grinding hulls. The workshops which handled heavier jobs, like metal rolling and forging were towards the Malin Bridge end of the valley; while the lighter trades of cutlery, razors and saws were further up the valley. The Rivelin Valley had dams squeezed into every feasible site and, when in its prime, there were about 20 dams supplying many more water wheels.

There is a small collection of pubs in the area, mostly old and each a fair way from the next. In fact, the first two that I am going to mention are so far along the river, going towards its source, that the river has been reduced to little more than a tiny brook.

The Surrey Arms, Manchester Road

This pub has been closed for a long time and I am not really sure about its location. I believe that it was situated in a farmhouse; that it would have been a beer-house catering for the passing travellers, or as it is fairly near to the Rivelin Dams, perhaps it served the needs of the navvies, imported to work on the dams' construction.

It would probably have been named after the Earl of Surrey and Arundel, a title taken by the heir to the Dukes of Norfolk.

There is a farm known as Surrey Farm a long way along Manchester Road just before Hollow Meadows Hospital. This could well have been the pub. Records have the Greaves family as licensees from 1833, Mary; 1841, Thomas and 1849, Hannah.

The Norfolk Arms, Manchester Road

I have been unable to locate this pub on a map of 1901, so I have no idea when it first opened, but I am sure that it was much earlier than that. It is situated opposite the Rivelin Dams so would have provided strong drink for the navvies working there. It is not inconceivable that this pub opened at about the same time as The Surrey Arms.

It was a very popular pub with walkers passing by and it used to be, perhaps still is, the terminus for buses running out from Sheffield. Nowadays, for some reason, perhaps a good refurbishing, it has added "New" to its name.

The Holly Bush, Hollins Lane

There is mentioned on a licensing document, dated 1841, in the Bradfield Parish archives, a Hollins Tavern. This could be The Holly Bush, as it is situated in Hollins Lane, just off Rivelin Valley Road. The landlord at this time was Isaac Bradwell; in 1849, the landlord was John Topham. The fairly modern detached building of today is a replacement for the original  pub building. I think that at one time, but many years ago, it sported a bowling green, but this has gone the way of most greens and become a carpark.

The Rivelin Hotel (Tavern), Tofts Lane

A villager, Isaac Baxter, who was a farmer and table knife blade grinder, applied for a licence for a Rivelin Tavern in 1857. The pub was open a few years before that. Standing as it does on the top edge of Tofts Lane, it looks out over the fields which drop away to the Rivelin Valley Road and is easy to spot. To aid this, although it is fading away now, it once had the name of the pub painted on the roof.

last orders

CHAPTER FIFTEEN
THE VILLAGES OF DORE AND TOTLEY

Situated to the south east of Sheffield, the two ancient villages of Dore and Totley are regarded by many people who live in the less salubrious parts of the city as the places where the "rich" people live.

This opinion is not without some foundation for the almost rural areas which make up these two villages are steeped in a feeling of well organised and quietly prosperous lives backed up by solid, if discreet, wealth. Many of the houses are large and detached and sit in large, well groomed gardens. The streets have litter swept from them in the summer and dead leaves in the winter. Here the city council cares; here lies influence more powerful than anyone living on a council estate can wield. As they say, it's not what you know, but who you know that counts!

This isn't a book of heavy to digest history; no dates to learn here, nor battles to remember, so it is more than enough to merely mention historic events which are connected to these villages.

This is an old area historically. The moorland which stretches away into Derbyshire laps at the fringes of the villages, indeed they were once part of Derbyshire, and has, over the years, yielded much evidence of ancient habitation. These are thought, by the people who study these things, to date back to c1000 BC. This information blends well with the old stone built houses which, while being in no way so old, form the village skeletons around which, especially in Dore, the newer parts have been crafted.

In Dore, on the swathe of grass which is called the village green, beside a memorial which remembers the war dead of the village, which was unveiled in 1932 beside another memorial to the Crimean War, there is a third memorial. This one unique. It is made from a piece of stone got from Stoke Hall, Grindleford and which weighs a ton and a half. Inset into the grey face of the stone is a piece of black Scottish granite which is shaped like a Saxon shield. Upon this is engraved the Golden Dragon of Wessex together with the words which tell of what happened at this spot. The memorial was designed by Mr R Eldon Minns.

The events which occurred here so long ago were recorded probably by the monks of Beauchief Abbey and these writings are today, so I have been told, lodged in the British Museum.

In 827 AD, Ecbert (or Ecgbert), King of Wessex and Mercia, met King Eanred of Northumbria to discuss the future governing of England. In 825 AD, Ecbert had defeated the army of Mercia in battle thus making his Kingdoms of Wessex, and now Mercia, the most powerful single force in the country. He had subsequently been accepted as overall ruler of the country by all the other territorial leaders, except Northumbria. To avoid a trial of strength between these two leaders, a meeting was needed. This victory and acceptance by the other leaders would have meant that Ecbert was in a very strong position during any bargaining; the King of Northumbria would have been after the best deal that he could get, short of going into battle.

This place was chosen as it was roughly on the border between their two kingdoms. What transpired at this meeting is not known, but when it finished, King Ecbert had been proclaimed King of All England. It must be remembered, of course, that the "England" of those days bore little resemblance to the country that we live in today.

Ecbert, who seems to be the first English king about which much is known, did manage to hang on to the crown for the following twelve years. Following his death, he was succeeded by his son, Ethelwulf, who reigned for 19 years. When he died, the succession for the next four kings consisted solely of his four sons - Ethelbald, Ethelbert, Ethelred and finally, Alfred the Great. Whether Alfred really was Great, I don't know, but I do know that he was 22 years old when he came to the throne and that he reigned for an eventful 28 years and is one of the few early English kings that everyone remembers.

Almost 200 years later, the Duke of Normandy, William, known to his friends, although out of earshot, as "William the Bastard", invaded England and won in battle what had been promised him anyway, the crown of England. This was in 1066. A few years later, as a sort of inventory of his kingdom, he commissioned the compiling of the two volume Domesday Book. This historic book gives details of both the small settlements of Dore and Totley. I'm not sure if Sheffield is mentioned.

Previous to 1935, when the Derbyshire villages of Dore and Totley were absorbed into South Yorkshire and became suburbs of Sheffield, the county border for some distance was Limb Brook. This insignificant watercourse springs into life just beside the hamlet of Ringinglow, wanders down the edge of Ecclesall Woods until it passes beneath Abbeydale Road and empties its small waters into the River Sheaf. It is one of several streams nearby which help to swell the river from which Sheffield took its name. Limb Brook probably got its name from the old word "lemo", meaning a place with elm trees. Before Dutch elm disease destroyed them, there were a large number of wych elms along the line of the brook.

Since the amalgamation with Sheffield, Dore and Totley, like most of the city's outlying areas, have grown apace and it is now becoming difficult to separate them. Totley is different from Dore in one respect though - it has more pubs.

There are three pubs in Dore still open:-

The Hare and Hounds, Church Lane

This is the oldest pub still open and it stands in the oldest part of the village. There used to be another licenced premises opposite, but this, it is believed, was bought by the landlord of The Hare and Hounds and closed down. One way to cope with the opposition - if you can afford it! An early landlord was Henry Elliott who was there in 1841 and 1849.

The Dore Moor Inn, Hathersage Road

This was built as an inn by James Wagstaffe to take advantage of the passing trade when the Chapel en le Frith toll road was opened. It dates back to the early 19th century and has recently been extended and modernised. At the time of writing this (1999), I believe that more work is planned. It is situated, as it's name suggests, in a bleak and windswept position, but pleasant.

The Devonshire Arms, High Street

This was formerly a beer-house. It is one of the many local public houses which have done and still do bear this name. It shows the large influence that this ducal house has had on the Sheffield area for many years.

It was built c1770 beside the site of a water trough which was fed by a nearby spring to cater for the large number of horses used in those palmy days. Like The Dore Moor Inn it has been altered and modernised, but externally it appears much as it has always done - granite walled and solid. In 1992, the brewery owners renovated a barn which stood at the rear of the pub to enlarge the bar space available.

There used to be a public house, a beer-house I suspect, known as, or most probably nicknamed, The Hogg's Den. This stood in a hollow above Whirlow Bridge, so is nothing really to do with Dore; all that is left of the building, which is believed to have housed the pub, are some crumbling pieces of wall. A man named Oates transferred the licence to a thatched cottage at Nether Causeway and thence to the centre of Dore village opposite The Hare and Hounds. This could have been the pub mentioned earlier as being closed down by its rival across the road. I have no solid proof of this, only the odd snippet of information that I have gleaned from various sources.

As I mentioned earlier, Totley boasts a richer vein of public houses than does Dore:-

The Crown, Hillfoot Road

Converted from three workmens cottages in the early 18th century, this pub was run by the Dalton family from at least 1813, when it was known locally as "Dorothy Dalton's". She and her husband were tenants of Lord Middleton and she was born in Totley in c1791. He husband, George, died in the 1830's leaving her to run the pub until her eldest son, Thomas, took over. He was also a firebrick maker and dealer possibly of Totley Moor. Dorothy was still there in 1841; her son in 1849.

At one time, the pub was one of the regular meeting places for the nearby Barlow Hunt, but after 1936, they must have gone elsewhere because from that day on they never met there again.

The Lords' Middleton, mentioned above, were created in 1711, during the reign of Queen Anne. The present baron is either the 12th or 13th.

The Fleur de Lys (or Lis), Totley Hall Lane

Although this pub site is probably not quite as old as The Crown, it is not far short. The name could well be derived from the coat of arms of the local Barker family, who once lived at nearby Totley Hall. It is not beyond the bounds of possibility that the family actually once owned the pub. The name could also come from the royal coat of arms which has incorporated the "lily flower" since the days of King Edward III. He was, for a short time and very tenuously, King of France, or part of it. Earlier this century, a small cattle market used to be held beside the pub and there was the village pinfold, where stray animals were impounded, behind the pub buildings. All very rural!

Early landlords were:- John Green, 1833 and 1849; Tom Kirby, 1919.

A new pub was built on the original site in 1933 and this is a mock Tudor-style building - very popular at the time among both house and pub architects. There are several dozen pubs of this style in Sheffield.

The Cricket Inn, Penny Lane

First mentioned in a trade directory of 1865. This records the landlord as being William Green. During the following 30 years, some of the landlords were:- John Coates, 1868; William Barker, 1876; William Anthony, 1879; Samuel Duncan, 1884; John Ashton, 1888-1894. This was the time that it took the Totley Tunnel to be built.

During a small pox epidemic, which struck down many of the navvies working on the tunnel, whose arrival and subsequent custom must have delighted every landlord in the vicinity, The Cricket Inn had a room, now I believe called The Barn Room, which was used as a "laying out" place for the dead bodies before they were removed to be buried in Dore Churchyard. These graves when full were marked, and they can still be seen today, "S.P.FULL UP".

When the tunnel was completed in 1894, there is no record of the pub for the following two years. The name, of course, is taken from the cricket pitch beside the pub buildings. Stand on the cricket field, absorb the view and the surroundings and it is amazing to be so near to the bustle of a large city.

The Grouse Inn, Penny Lane

The landlord in 1872 was Clement Needham, he was there for many years. At this time it was known as a beer-house. During the construction of the Totley Tunnel, it is believed that large numbers of these men lodged at the pub following the shrewd action by Mr Needham, who built a large extension at the front of the pub to accommodate them.

The towels went over the pumps for the final time in 1956 and the building became the private house that it remains today.

The name of the pub, of course, fits in perfectly with the large expanse of grouse moor which is near the pub.

The Ye Olde Crossed Scythes, Baslow Road

Part of the buildings which make up this well documented pub are believed to be c300 years old. In the beginning of the 19th century, a local land owner, George Greaves, rented out some farm buildings to Samuel Hopkinson, who was both a local farmer and scythemaker. This duality of trades was common in those days, especially when one of the trades involved dependence on water power which could fail during a long, hot summer.

When the Baslow to Sheffield turnpike was built, Mr Hopkinson opened a beer-house in the farm buildings to cash in on the "halfway" position that the buildings enjoyed between Baslow and Sheffield. He is recorded as being the landlord in 1833; in 1836, the landlord was Thomas Fisher, also a farmer. He was followed by John Thorpe in 1846 who had the pub for 10 years and altered the name from The Crossed Scythes Inn to The Ye Olde Crossed Scythes. He gained the reputation for being a "local character", whatever that means. He was very popular and died on a visit to Dublin, aged 75 years. He was buried in Dore churchyard along with his two sons.

Two other early landlords were John Wagstaff and Job Green. Mr Green was a well known local man, who was involved in the new Totley Chapel. He stayed at the pub until c1868, dying five years later. The last of the early landlords listed in trades directories was Thomas Bown, the son of a coal miner. He was also a busy man being listed as a blacksmith and agricultural implement maker. He would have used the smithy, which adjoined the pub buildings, but which has now been demolished. This smithy would have been a big draw when the turnpike road was in operation - no-one could go far if the horse's shoes needed attention.

In 1885, a Grimesthorpe haulage contractor, Michael Cottam, started up a horse-drawn bus service between the pub and the Dore and Totley railway station, about 1¹/₂ miles.

Until the local Roman Catholics found a permanent home in 1964, the newly built Church of the English Martyrs, for about eight years they held services in part of the pub buildings.

The name today has reverted to simply The Cross Scythes and is still a bus terminus.

The Green Oak Inn, Baslow Road

According to George Greaves, mentioned earlier, giving a statement at the Enclosure Enquiry held at the Old Schoolhouse, Totley Hall Lane in 1839, this pub was built about this time. It is possible, however, that there was an older building on the site previous to this date, but whether this was a pub is not possible to ascertain. There is a landlord listed in 1833 called Samuel Biggin.

The Green Oak was probably built, like the nearby Crossed Scythes, to take advantage of the new turnpike road. Samuel Biggin was one of the few landlords and he was followed by Charles Vickers. Mr Vickers and his wife were both born locally. He was also a farmer. He rented about 22 acres of land and some buildings from George Greaves (Mr Greaves seems to have been both a wealthy and influential man in Totley in those days) and he remained in the pub until moving to Rycroft Farm, Dore in c1850. Following Mr Vickers departure, the pub closed and it is next mentioned in records as Green Oak House.

The pub used to be located beside the Green Oak toll-bar and cottage. Today it can be located as being on the opposite side of the road from the junction of Baslow Road with Mickley Lane. Here there is a row of shops - The Busy Bee, then an archway, then a greengrocers. This shop was the site of The Green Oak Inn, or so I have been told by the local author and artist, Brian Edwards.

The Peacock, Owler Bar

The inn appears to have been built at the same time as the first toll-bar. It was originally known as

The Owler Bar Inn. When the name was changed to The Peacock, it seems logical to suppose that this name was taken from part of the coat of arms of the landlord, The Duke of Rutland, who owned the grouse moors around the inn.

The Owler Bar Inn, c1900

In the 1860's, when the tenant of the inn was William Coates, Owler Bar was well known for holding pony trotting races. These died out at the end of the 19th century when they were deemed to be a danger to the public. It seems that they were even more dangerous to the ponies involved! Mr Coates owned a pony called Blazing Bob. This pony was one day, no doubt for a bet, driven to Manchester and back. This is a mighty long distance for a trotting pony to cover in one stint. It bravely managed to do it, but dropped dead a few minutes after arriving home. Like I've said - they made their own entertainment in those days!

When the toll-bar was abolished and the last toll collected in 1888, the pub remained. It was a well known coaching house and then, in the late 1880's, two coaches a day called there. One was painted yellow and was known as The Enterprise; the other was painted red and known as Lucy Long. They served Matlock and Buxton. The inn could well have been the first stop to change horses on either journey.

William Broughton took over the licence in 1884. He was a well known hay and straw dealer. This was the start of a long period of occupation by this family. When William died in 1903, his widow ran the pub for 20 years until 1923, when her son, John, became landlord. He bought the lease from The Duke of Rutland in 1927.

CHAPTER SIXTEEN
THE ABBEYDALE AREA

This is a difficult area to cover, stretching as it does mostly along the length of Abbeydale Road. It has never been an actual village, more a collection of buildings straggling down the valley. It was here that the monks from Beauchief Abbey began their early ironworks and it is from this abbey that the area takes its name. It doesn't have many pubs, but what few it does have are old and well known. There are also several historic sites which I thought were well worth writing about.

The Licenced Victuallers Almshouses and Memorial

The Sheffield, Rotherham & District Licenced Victuallers Association Benevolent Institution (Asylum) boasted not only a long and ungainly title, but was also founded on August 1st, 1844, aided by donations from Alderman Thomas Wiley, for the "reception, maintenance and support of aged, distressed and unfortunate licenced victuallers" who belonged to the Association. It was no doubt a very worthy cause, but I can't help thinking that people who had spent their working lives, especially in the centuries gone by, when the working classes quite often existed on mere subsistence wages, selling the strong drink which wrecked many a man's life and with it his family's, didn't deserve too much sympathy when they too fell on hard times. Perhaps I am wrong.

The almshouses were originally situated in Grimesthorpe, where seven houses, designed by ME Hadfield in Tudor-style, were built for that purpose from May 17th, 1848 onwards. The memorial to the good alderman, dated 1853, was first erected there and, when the asylum moved to Abbeydale, it was re-erected there in 1879. The inscription on the stonework of the memorial gives a detailed description of the events.

The present site was subsequently bought and a foundation stone laid by Lord Cavendish, a scion of the Dukes of Devonshire, on June 6th, 1877. The twelve houses, which include two semi-detached villas and a central boardroom, were opened on July 24th, 1879 by the Rt. Hon. Arthur Roebuck MP. These were designed in late Gothic-style by JB Mitchell-Withers. The total cost of the buildings was £13,000.

At the turn of the century, each widower and widow, or married couple, occupied a separate house. The former received £22/2s/0^D (£22.10) and the latter £32/10s/0^D (£32.50) a year for life together with coal, gas and the use of a plot of land for growing vegetables. Although the sum allowed per year only amounted to about 8s/6^D (42^1/2p) a week for a single person and 12s/6^D (62^1/2p) a week for a married couple, when the security of a warm dwelling and the other fringe benefits were added, it wasn't a bad situation to be in.

Don't let us forget that then there were no old age pensions, they didn't arrive until 1909, and the usual thing, if a person couldn't still work and maintain themselves and their family couldn't have them, was a bed in the local workhouse - a prospect viewed by all old people with terror!

During the First World War, 1914-1918, the almshouses served as an auxiliary hospital. There were many of these scattered throughout the country due to the immense numbers of wounded and gassed servicemen returning from the trenches in France and the other theatres of the war.

The properties are now owned by a local Freemasons Society and called Woodland View.

The Church of St. John the Evangelist and Church Rooms

Not far away from the almshouses, opposite the Abbeydale Sports Club, stands the church of St. John the Evangelist. It was built with the financial support of John Roberts Esq., who was a silversmith and who lived at nearby Abbeydale Hall. It was consecrated by the Bishop of Lichfield on January 11th, 1876. The cost of building this pleasantly English style of church was £5,922 and it incorporated a chancel, a nave, a vestry and an organ chamber. The parish it serves today was formed in January, 1878.

In 1926, a baptistry containing three memorial windows to a Mrs Kerfoot was built to celebrate the church's golden jubilee. The church was enlarged again in 1937 at a cost of some £4,000 by the addition of two side aisles. This added a further 120 seats to the former capacity of 220 seats. A lady chapel and a childrens' corner were also added.

A local man, Ebenezer Hall, a friend of John Roberts, who followed him in living at Abbeydale Hall, together with his wife, were responsible, by means of a donation of £3,000 in 1893, for the creation of the adjacent church rooms which stand to the right of the church. These were built in what may be called English Gothic style with a small tower, fine stonework and attractive windows.

These church rooms were pressed into service during the First World War and served as a Voluntary Aid Detachment (VAD) hospital. This fact is commemorated by a very fine mosaic, still predominantly golden, above the main entrance doors. This depicts a nurse on one side, a soldier on the other while in the centre, above the inscription, is a clock. This, I believe, was unveiled in the early 1920's.

The building was purchased by the Post Office from the Parochial Church Council in 1956 and is now used, rather unfortunately, as a postal sorting office. Better than dereliction, I suppose.

The Abbeydale Industrial Hamlet

The reason that the Abbeydale Industrial Hamlet, as it is known today, is where it is was because of the water power available from the nearby River Sheaf. The same reason applies to many of the old industrial areas of Sheffield - The Loxley and Rivelin valleys are good examples.

This was one of the largest water powered sites along the River Sheaf and its main products were the large edge tools, which were used mainly in agriculture and horticulture. Several types of scythes, grass hooks of many shapes and sizes, hay cutting knives and even hand shears for sheep shearing. These are a good cross-section of the products made there. It must be remembered that each agricultural district in England had its own needs and preferences when selecting the tools they needed. Some districts liked a completely different size and shape of grass hook than did another. Tradition probably.

Although the earliest actual records of the site date back only to 1714, there was an industry of an early type in the near vicinity from as far back as the 13th century when the Beauchief monks operated a smithy on the opposite side of the river. For "modern" industry, the most probable accurate date is 1685, when Hugh Stephenson rented a waterwheel here.

The all important mill dam was enlarged in 1777 and this was followed by many additional industrial facilities being added to the site to take advantage of the extra water power. The tilt hammer forge was built in 1785; cottages to house the increased number of workmen employed were erected in 1793, and in 1817, the grinding hull was built.

To cater for the raw material used on the site, mostly steel, a crucible furnace was built in c1830 together with a number of other buildings to serve as offices, hand forges and a warehouse. Later on in the 19th century, various stabling and a managers house were added. The crucible furnace, once one of a huge number in Sheffield, is very likely the only one of its kind left in a fit condition to operate.

During the 18th and 19th centuries, this group of old, but well preserved industrial workshops, forges, offices and houses, some of which are now Grade II listed and I believe that one is Grade I listed, standing on the site of a much earlier lead smelting works, was a noisy, smoky, bustling and profitable place which employed a large number of local craftsmen.

The hamlet stands just below the water level of the adjoining mill dam, which supplied the motive force which operated the majority of the machinery in the forges and workshops. These included the huge trip hammers used to shape hot metal and the grindstones to further shape and hone the edges of the tools. These old pieces of industrial history are still, following restoration work, fit to operate.

In 1842, due to the industrial problems caused by Dyson's Ltd, the operating company, employing non-union labour, the grinding hull was badly damaged when a charge of gunpowder was set off inside. This was the work of the militant Grinder's Union. The usual method employed in these cases was to drop a bag of the explosive down the chimney. That seemed to work pretty well!

In the late 19th century, the hamlet stopped regular production and the firm which had been the tenants of the site since c1849, Tyzack & Sons Ltd, moved down the road to their other, more modern works at Little London.

It was, however, not quite the end of the road for the hamlet, for the crucible furnace was once again fired up during the Second World War to help to supply the much needed steel.

The well known businessman and benefactor, JG Graves, had bought the site in 1935 and given it to the city. It was restored and handed over to the Sheffield Museums Department. They opened it to the public in 1970.

Unfortunately, due to political and economic reasons, the hamlet was closed to the public in March, 1997 and although it did reopen briefly for seven weeks in 1998, the future at that time looked bleak; many loyal and regular visitors to the hamlet were aghast at what they considered to be yet another short-sighted decision by the City Council.

Things have since improved. Although the hamlet is still owned by the City Council, a trust has been set up, The Sheffield Industrial Museums Trust. They have leased the site from the council and will manage, and hopefully, develop it. They can hardly make a bigger mess of running it than did the council. In 2000, it has been open quite often.

The following four public houses are all still in business and all are very popular:-

The Millhouses, Abbeydale Road

This used to be known as The Millwright Arms. In an 1845 trade directory, it was recorded as being a beer-house. It is probable that there was a workshop and a smithy beside the pub, the site of which is now the pub carpark. This tragic necessity was laid down in 1958, when the pub was heavily refurbished and the old outbuildings knocked down.

It is very unusual to be able to trace back the dates of occupation of a long list of landlords of a particular pub. It is easy to pore over the trade directories, as you will notice throughout this book, I do it frequently, but this merely gives the landlord of the year that the directory covers. He, or she, could have been there for many years, or they tenure could have been very short. Only by searching through a whole series of consecutive directories can the length of time be worked out. This I have tried and I have decided that life is far too short for this sort of research!

In the bar of The Millhouses, surrounded by fine old photographs of both the pub and its surroundings in bygone days, there is a framed list of all the landlords, and one landlady, who have presided in this pub right back to 1883.

This I have copied:-

Sarah Brown - 1883 to 1902;	Edward Shaw Horton - 1902 to 1907;
Henry Alfred Bowater - 1907 to 1922;	Thomas Alfred Badger - 1922 to 1938;
Joseph Thomas Badger - 1938 to 1956;	William Douthwaite - 1956 to 1962;
Cornelius Aherne - 1962 - 1973;	Ronald Lawrence - 1973 to 1977;
James Finch - 1977 to 1985;	John French - 1985 to 1988;
Graham Burke - 1988 to 1991;	Stephen Charles Nichols - 1991 to 1994;
Michael Charles Gent - 1995 to 1999.	

An earlier landlord in 1845 was Joshua Hodgkinson, who was also a millwright. It seems likely that his son, William, took over the licence as he is recorded as being landlord in 1864.

I must say, having recorded all this richness of information, that while it is interesting, it is not all that important. Who, except perhaps distant relatives, really cares who kept a pub over 100 years ago? Is it of any particular historical value? I think not. To be honest, which I often am, I am quite glad that I don't encounter statistics like this in every pub that I write about. I would feel compelled to include them in any description that I wrote and while this might help to "pad out" some of the sketchy bits when I haven't been able to find much of interest about a certain pub, put a number of these descriptions together and the result would be verging on just a mass of names and dates. It is possible to get too much of a good thing.

The Robin Hood, Millhouses Lane

Formerly known as The Robin Hood and Little John. In a directory of 1825, the landlady was Ann Lingard; in 1841, Ann Dowling, who mixed running a pub with raising six children. Later, in 1851, she became a school mistress and one of her sons became the headmaster of a school. In 1849, Eneas Brown, who

was also a coal owner, was landlord until his death. The pub was then taken over by his widow, Mrs Brown. She was also a brickmaker - two tough jobs for an obviously tough lady! The pub stayed in the Brown family until 1919 when Duncan Gilmour's Brewery bought it. Presumably, before that it was a free-house, probably a beer-house.

The Waggon and Horses, Abbeydale Road South

Originally a farmhouse, part of this pub was built by dressed stone taken from a mill dam, which used to be at the junction of Totley Brook and Old Hay Brook and which was demolished at the turn of the last century.

The following account of the life of the mill site has little to do with The Waggon and Horses, but is interesting enough to include, as it shows a little about the industry which used to thrive in this area.

The mill was there at least as early as 1615; it began as a lead smelting works and in 1750, part of it was converted to serve as a cutlers' grinding wheel. Sold in 1759, by 1780 a lead rolling mill was constructed on the site. In 1836, it was bought by the Abbeydale Works scythe maker, John Dyson, for rolling steel; plus part of the site was used for lead smelting.

In a directory of 1825, the landlord of this pub was James Smith. He was also a woodman. This trade was probably, in this area, involved in the management of the nearby Ecclesall Woods. In the olden days there were many more uses for wood than there are today and coppicing was an important part of a woodman's job. This is the cutting down of a mature tree, then the regular harvesting of the young shoots which grew around the stump. In 1841, the landlady of the pub was Mary Gill and, until 1871, William and Mary Smith.

I recently managed to find out much more about the modern pub when I met Mrs Thelma Coy. The pub was bought by Courages from Trust Houses in about 1967 and when she and her late husband Fred, moved in as managers, in July '67, a full refurbishment programme was in full swing. This was so extensive that they were forced to live off the premises until the major part of it had been completed. This work formed the basis of how the pub looks today.

Following the early death of her husband, Mrs Coy left the pub in September, 1973 and took The Cuthbert Arms, Langsett Road, moving in on 1st November, 1973. This was a typical small, Sheffield beerhouse with a "beer-off" at the front, which originally held the beer-pump which supplied the beer to the small bar at the rear. Owned by John Smith's Brewery, it was closed in 1975 and later, along with many adjoining buildings, demolished.

The Beauchief Hotel, Abbeydale Road South / Abbey Lane

This is a large, detached and imposing Victorian building which was once the station buildings for Abbeydale Station - a fact which is still to be seen in granite letters above what used to be the main door of the hotel. Until recently this could fairly have been described as a public house, but now it has a large extension to the rear and although there are bars, they are there more to cater for the restaurant customers, rather than any "public bar" trade. Across Abbey Lane, where there is today a petrol filing station, there used to be the railway sidings and where the hotel carpark is now used to be the bowling green and also an orchard - both buried for ever beneath tarmac and white lines.

I thought that it might be a good idea to add a small piece here about Bradway. This small hamlet is now a prosperous suburb of Sheffield and has a collection of four pubs, all popular and two have unusual, perhaps, unique names:-

The Old Mother Redcap, Prospect Road, Poynton Wood

This is a very new pub, designed for crowds and built to cater for people from the new houses and small estates nearby, which it seems to do very well, although there has not been enough time since this pub was built for it to build up any atmosphere. Externally I don't think that I have ever seen a pub, new or old, which is so unprepossesing. It has as much character as a council rent office. I could have photographed it but I didn't bother

The name is interesting. Old Mother Red Cap could have two meanings. I'm not sure that either are correct. Often it was applied to a woman who was as keen on beer as any man - an ale wife or it could mean an elderly buffer girl. These tough ladies always wore a red scarf around their heads. It was so common that it became a badge of office and was worn with pride. Additionally, I have also heard that the name applies to a witch.

The Shepley Spitfire, Mickley Lane

The name of this pub is far easier to explain. A young man named Douglas Shepley, served in the RAF during the Second World War, and was a fighter pilot flying Spitfires. He was, like so many of these brave young men, only 21 years old when he died. It was during the early days of the Battle of Britain that he was shot down and killed. I believe that it occurred while he was involved in a "dog fight" with several German planes over the English Channel. It was August 12th, 1940.

His family, which included his young wife of only a few weeks, began a collection to find the money to build a replacement Spitfire. It was an action which was common in those black days when Britain had her back to the wall. They succeeded and a plane called The Shepley Spitfire was built. It too was destroyed by enemy fire, but luckily this time the young pilot escaped with his life to fight again.

The pub was opened in 1979 and architecturally it is almost like a bungalow. Like The Old Mother Redcap, it serves the surrounding little housing estates.

The Castle Inn, Twentywell Road

This is a 19th century pub site which began life as one of a terrace of similar small houses. It was later to spread to an adjoining house which now forms part of the enlarged pub. I have heard that these cottages were built to accommodate the gangs of navvies who arrived to build the Bradway railway tunnel. Today it is a pleasantly secluded little pub well worth a visit.

The Bradway Hotel, Bradway Road

This is probably the oldest pub in the area and it began its life probably as a beer-house to cater again for the navvies. In those days and for many years after, it was known as The Miners Inn (or Arms). Many of the navvies working on this project were not simply pick and shovel labourers, but skilled miners hence the pub's name.

The pub was replaced in the 1920's with the building which stands today, another mock Tudor effort. The pub's name changed a few years ago. I have a feeling that architecturally this building looks uneasily out of place here.

CHAPTER SEVENTEEN
ECCLESALL

Lying below which I describe in the next chapter as The Western Suburbs, is the large district which can be given the general heading of "Ecclesall". There never was an actual village of Ecclesall. In the 17th and 18th centuries the township consisted of a number of loosely connected hamlets and farms joined by a network of rough tracks and lanes. A township was the smallest unit of local government in those days - now it is a parish. Bierlow, as in Ecclesall Bierlow, was the Danish equivalent of township. The name of Ecclesall very possibly comes from the old words for witches' slope or witches' hill, "Hecksel-Hallr".

Ecclesall is not mentioned in The Domesday Book, but there is an historically important family, the de Ecclesalls', who are first recorded in c1200. This family had much to do with Beauchief Abbey.

This area has the long and serpentine Ecclesall Road as a roughly central spine. Running from right to left and mostly in a southwest direction, this road begins where Hanover Road meets St. Mary's Gate and Moore Street. It ends at Whirlow and along its length there are several interesting places.

Going away from Sheffield, on the left hand side of the road, just after the now defunct Sheaf Brewery of SH Ward & Co, down a side street, is the General Cemetery.

This was opened in 1836 and was the first burial ground in Sheffield that wasn't a churchyard. It was a private company founded to make money as well as to bury the dead. According to a booklet published by the Friends of the General Cemetery, a very worthy organisation, the reason that the new, large cemetery was so desperately needed was due to the chronic overcrowding in the local churchyards. This was so bad that there were accounts of "evil smelling fluids oozing through the churchyard walls"!

The six acres of the cemetery, bought from the snuff maker, Henry Wilson, were at first not too popular and in the first year there were only 19 burials. Perhaps this was because it cost more than did a churchyard burial. It is a pity that it didn't open a couple of years earlier; then the cholera epidemic would have boosted business no end! Business did pick up, however, and various local medical disasters are reflected in the figures. In 1888, there was a smallpox epidemic and there were 1,189 internments; in 1918, following a 'flu outbreak, there were 653.

When the cemetery finally closed in the 1930's, due to lack of grave space, it is estimated that there were c87,000 bodies buried in the site. Not everyone, of course, had a large and imposing tomb. Many of the poorer people were buried in public plots and it was common practice, in the 19th century when infant mortality was high, to bury babies "top to tail".

The council took control of the cemetery in 1977 and since then it has done very little to either improve this asset or even to maintain what they were given. One act which they did carry out has been described in another book as "an act of municipal vandalism on a huge scale"! This was the bulldozing flat and the removal of roughly a third of the tombstones in the cemetery. Some of these stones, bought and paid for by families, have, so I was once told by a retired works department worker, since been used to surface paths - face down, of course. I sometimes find the actions of Sheffield City Council completely incomprehensible!

Many well known people were buried in the cemetery - Samuel Holberry, the Chartist agitator; Mark Firth, the steel magnate; George Bassett, famous for his sweets; two of the Cole brothers.... the list is long. Other people were not well known. One stone commemorates a lady named Margaret Green, who was the mother of 10 children, all of whom died before the age of five years old. She was only 45 years old when she herself died. There is also the grave of a little lad named Herbert, who was only two years old in 1864 when he was drowned in the Great Flood.

All is not lost regarding the General Cemetery. The Friends labour long, hard and intelligently to claw it back from what once looked like becoming total dereliction. If you are interested in helping them, phone Jane on 255 6092.

Not much further along Ecclesall Road, down any one of several side streets on the right, are the Botanical Gardens. These were designed by Robert Marnock, of Regent's Park, London and opened to the public on June 29th, 1836, at a cost of about £20,000.

Initially, they were owned by the Sheffield Botanical and Horticultural Society and then the Town Trustees in 1951, when the then Sheffield Corporation took them over on a 99 year lease at an annual rental of 1/- (5p)per year.

Apart from a varied and well maintained collection of trees, flowers and shrubs, other features include the Crimean War Memorial, which used to stand at Moorhead and which was moved here to allow for road improvements. During the move, the council managed to lose two, eight foot long bronze cannon and a 17 foot high Aberdeen granite column. Undeterred as usual, they erected what remained.

The glass pavilions were the result of a design chosen by a panel of judges which included Sir Joseph Paxton. The bear pit used to house two bears, but was closed in 1870 following the death of a child, who allegedly fell into the pit and was clawed to death by the bears. It did open once more for a short period in the 19th century when the keeper of a performing bear was found drunk and incapable in the city centre. He went to jail, the bear went to the bear pit! The gardens have recently reopened following extensive refurbishment.

Going up Ecclesall Road towards Hunter's Bar, on the left hand side of the road is a narrow lane. It passes between a Pizza Hut and Thresher's off licence and it leads to one of Sheffield's hidden treasures - Sharrow Mills.

Not now a hugely popular pastime, but in past years, in the 18th and 19th centuries especially, the taking of a pinch of snuff was one of the great pleasures in life. It was a product used by every level of society - from labourers right up to kings.

The Wilson family were the leaders in snuff production in this country and even today still maintain a large share of the market.

Joseph Wilson, born in 1723, a silversmith, is generally recognised as the founder of this family firm when he came into possession of the secrets of how to make snuff. This was c1740. Ten years later, snuff making had taken over as the largest of his business interests and the water mill beside the Porter Brook had been converted into mainly a snuff mill, Sharrow Mills. As with most water powered trades, the grinding of snuff was very dependent on the levels of water in the dam and when it became available, the grinding machinery was turned over to steam power in 1797.

A rift between the family members led to a rival Wilson's snuff company being set up nearby at Westbrook Mill, Joseph & Henry Wilson Ltd, and for many years, until Westbrook Mill was taken over by the giant Imperial Tobacco Company in 1953, the two companies observed strict territorial boundaries and both survived in business. Westbrook Mill has now been closed and is offices.

Wilsons & Co (Sharrow) of Sharrow Mills still grinds on though and is still in the firm control of members of the Wilson family, although perhaps only by marriage.

The modern part of the mill complex today uses all the very latest technology, but in the old part of the mill, in the cellars, there is still the original waterwheel and upstairs in the old wooden rooms, steeped in both the dust and the smell of years old snuff and covered in a thick coat of brown snuff, is the original grinding equipment.

When I left the old darkness and gloom of the mill and walked out into the 20th century, I felt that I was leaving the Dickensian age behind me. More was to come, though. In a workshop in the corner of the mill's main cobbled yard is where the skilled hands of two ladies make clay-pipes. Dozens and dozens of various patterned clay-pipes, made with moulds many years old. No-one smokes them much today, but it seems that they have a steady trade with TV and film companies. The ladies gave me one, seeing that I was a pipe smoker - it burned my tongue!

Just past Hunter's Bar, now a traffic roundabout, but once a much hated tollgate, is Endcliffe Park. This covers nine acres and was bought by public subscription to commemorate the Golden Jubilee of Queen Victoria. It was placed in the care of the Corporation on the understanding that it would always remain a public park.

Today, it seems to be the dumping ground for various former city centre memorials. The statue of Queen Victoria, which was erected in Town Hall Square, amid much rejoicing, pomp and ceremony in 1905, is there, although almost smothered by trees, and so is the Golden Jubilee Oberlisk it replaced.

There is also a small plaque which remembers the crew of an American bomber, which crashed near there during the Second World War.

The park is divided by the small, meandering Porter Brook, which in its time has supported a number of waterwheels.

The actual boundaries of Ecclesall are difficult to determine and, to be honest, the road from the city to Whirlow offers more interesting attractions. All Saint's Church, in all its boxlike ugliness, is perched on a hill beside the road and is the centre of what is probably the most interesting and prestigious churchyard in Sheffield. Here, in the 19th century, was the place to be buried. Forget the General Cemetery; to be interred here was to be on top of the funerary pile! Sir John Brown; William Jessop; the Butcher brothers; many of the Wilson snuff family; Samuel Osborn; Arnold Loosemore VC; Henry Sorby; Sir Frederick Thorpe Mappin and a couple of bishops are to name just a few of the well known graves in this place.

The Whirlow Bridge Inn, Ecclesall Road South

c1890

In c1846, this was a beer-house, probably built about that date; it became known as The Bridge Inn in 1852, when the landlord was John Revill and then in 1895, The Whirlow Bridge Inn. The licence to sell intoxicating liquors was rescinded in the 1920's and the buildings were converted into a temperance tearooms (horror of horrors!) - probably much to the dismay of the regular customers. It became, however, a popular stop off for walkers and travellers. It had an attractive double frontage and its facilities were boosted by gardens and stables. To the rear of the buildings there was a dam with boats for hire. This dam, I have been told, is still in existance.

c1890

Following its closure as a business premises, it became a private house and was finally demolished in 1938. This was probably to allow for road straightening works to be carried out due to the increase in motor traffic.

The Wheatsheaf Inn, Ecclesall Road South

The original pub which stood on this site and which dated back to c1695, was demolished in 1928 to allow for the building of the pub which stands here today. There used to be a smithy, later a garage, beside the old pub. It was a popular stop on the way to Castleton.

One of the 19th century landlords, when the pub was probably only a beer-house, was Joseph Baker, who held the licence between at least 1825 to 1852.

The site now boasts a large, detached and modern hotel - too large for its position. There is more of an interest in the restaurant side of the business than in the public house side, a trend which is becoming more and more common.

The Hammer and Pincers, Ringinglow Road, Bents Green

This used to be a group of cottages which housed a smithy and were owned by a family of blacksmiths named Osborne. In the 1820's, part of the buildings were turned into a beer-house with Joseph Osborne as landlord. There is a Joseph Osborne listed as landlord between 1833 and 1849 and a Thomas Osborne in 1852.

It was situated on the old turnpike road and the combination of the smithy and the pub, together with the distance from Sheffield, would have ensured plenty of business. By 1958, the smithy had disappeared and the buildings were all used as the pub.

Although it is now owned by Bass Charrington's, in the years immediately after the Second World War, it was serving Mappin's beers. This was a smallish brewery based on the outskirts of Rotherham at Masbrough. It is not impossible that this pub was once called The Blacksmith's Arms.

Bear baiting, a cruel but popular sport in the 18th and 19th centuries, used to be held at the pub about once a year - a special treat, I suppose. This was discontinued when one of the bears got its own back and "worried" the landlord!

The Norfolk Arms, Ringinglow Road

Travel from where Ringinglow Road branches off from Ecclesall Road South, past Hill Top and then continue along the arrow straight part of Ringinglow Road and you will arrive at the tiny hamlet of Ringinglow. Perhaps I could just as well have included this pub in the Western Suburbs chapter.

There isn't much there, there never has been. A few houses, a chapel, an octagonal shaped former tollhouse known as the Round House, the source of Limb Brook which wanders away to join the River Sheaf at Abbeydale, a bus stop - and The Norfolk Arms. Travel a few hundred yards further and you will be in the Peak National Park; travel half a mile further and you will be in Derbyshire.

c1890

In 1758, when the principal road from Sheffield westwards to the High Peak and Manchester was first made into a turnpike, Ringinglow hamlet stood at the junction of the two ways to Buxton, via Fox House and to Chapel en le Frith, via Sparrowpit. For nearly 50 years this road had a monopoly of land transport between Manchester, High Peak and Sheffield and in its early days, the Trust that oversaw its operation seems to have prospered.

Despite this, a new Act was passed through parliament in 1795, allowing the Trust to raise the tolls demanded and to build new tollbars, including one where "the roads branch off from each other at the guide post near Barker's Fields Cupola to Sparrowpit Lane and Buxton". That is, at Ringinglow. The Act also permitted "the

building of a tollhouse and suitable outbuildings and the enclosing of a suitable garden plot out of adjoining wasteland, not exceeding one rood (a quarter of an acre) in area". This must have been done by the end of 1795 as the tollhouse appears on Fairbank's Parish Map of the same year.

modern view

I do not know why the tollhouse was built as an octagon, or the reason for providing a loft which has never had any windows or a solid floor. I do not believe that there were at this time similar looking examples of tollhouses or other buildings in this area, although the combination of Gothic windows, quatrefoils and battlements also appeared on Huntsman's Forge (about 1780) beside Lady's Bridge and later on the canal tollhouse at Tinsley Locks (1819). Gothic was not, I believe, used in churches or country houses around here for another 25 years.

The Norfolk Arms, built by Rawson's Brewery, Pond Street, shortly afterwards in c1803, was crenellated to match and the long dead newspaper, The Northern Star, commented in 1819 on the two buildings saying "their being castellated as though they marked some important barrier".

Two early licensees were:- Mary Whitworth in 1841 and Charles Marsden, of the well known Marsden family, in 1849 and 1852.

Ringinglow Bar became almost the most lucrative on the road realising £421 in 1797/1798. This sum was only bettered, rather surprisingly, by the Handsworth Tollbar. The opening of rival roads, more direct and with easier gradients, in the early years of the 19th century, reduced Ringinglow's importance as a road junction and in 1825, both roads were demoted to parish highway status and the tollhouse was sold off. By 1840, it formed part of the estate of Rawson's Brewery, owner of The Norfolk Arms.

The reason that this pub was built in such an isolated place was obviously to supply the needs of the travellers using the turnpike. As the only pub for quite a large area, it was also a meeting place for farmers, grouse shooting parties and hikers who were either walking out towards Hathersage or back towards Sheffield. All in all, it was a shrewd place to build a pub. Perhaps that is why Rawson's Brewery were in business for almost 200 years before being bombed in December, 1940!

I know little else about the pub, apart from a landlord sometime in the 19th century being Henry Broomhead. He lived between 1823 and 1900. He was a member of another well known Mayfield family and was related by marriage to the Marsdens.

In the pub carpark there is an old milestone still standing and set into the wall beside the pub is a rare Victorian postbox. The front of the pub is where many of the buses turn round before heading back down Ringinglow Road towards Sheffield.

There are two tales to tell here. One relates to the pub and one to Ringinglow hamlet. The first I think may be true; the second I don't.

In April, 1876, at a time when there was a dearth of news to print in the local newspapers (there were several in those days), commonly known in the trade as "slow news days", two journalists from rival newspapers fabricated a nice little hoax in a bid to boost newspaper sales.

An advertising placard appeared in prominent places in the town which read,

"Horrid Murder At Ringinglow!!" This caused a stir among the passers-by who read it. People, after all, love tragedies, providing it doesn't personally affect themselves! The rival journalist, not to be outdone, issued his own placard. It read, "Body Found!!"

Then as now, people couldn't wait to get onto the fringes of something nasty and many set off to walk to Ringinglow - a matter of several miles - hoping, at least, to catch a glimpse of a bloodstained body. As there was nothing to see, and after wandering around the desolate moors searching for non-existent clues, the people did the natural thing and piled into the bar of The Norfolk Arms. The landlord, a Mr Garratt, was waiting for them, ready to rake in the money hand over fist!

Was the landlord in league with the two journalists? Were the two journalists in league with each other? Who knows! It wasn't a bad business ploy, though. Even if it could only be used once.

The second tale purports to give the reason for the name of hamlet, Ringinglow. "One dark and stormy night", as they say, during an 18th century winter, a man from Sheffield was returning home across the moors and he became hopelessly lost. Half dead with cold and despair he had just about given himself up for lost when, in the far distance and just barely discernable, he heard the sound of the bells of Sheffield Parish Church. He followed the direction of the sound "ringing low in the valley" and finally arrived exhausted in the town.

A wealthy man, he realised that it was the sound of the bells that had saved his life and he donated a sum of money to be divided between the bell-ringers on that same night every year.

That, so the legend claims, is why that stretch of moorland and the hamlet are called "Ringinglow". I don't believe a word of it. After all, if he was that wealthy, why was he having to walk home?

After that, I won't even mention the ghost named Eric, who wears a cap and raincoat and who haunts The Norfolk Arms and becomes upset if a picture of The Laughing Cavalier, hanging somewhere inside the pub, is moved.

The Prince of Wales, Ecclesall Road South

c1920

Built in c1808, when it had tearooms and a bowling green, this pub was knocked down and rebuilt in 1928 in the popular mock Tudor-style. In the 1980's, it was revamped to form an American-style diner and renamed The Woodstock Diner - just what was needed in Ecclesall, I would have thought! By the early 1990's, its owners were still vainly chasing the supposed fashions of the day, and it was once again refurbished and renamed

The Real Macaw. It has, since 1996, reverted to its original and perfectly reasonable name, The Prince of Wales. Of course, it won't ever be the same. Two "modernisation" efforts in a handful of years has successfully removed any ambiance and atmosphere which had built up since 1928. When will they ever learn?

The early pub could well have been built from dressed stones taken from the remains of the old Ecclesall Chapel which used to stand on or near to the site of the present All Saints Church. It was very common in past centuries for the chapel or church to be near to the village pub.

Some early landlords of the pub were:- Robert Dent, 1825; G. Green, 1833; Thomas Walker, 1841, who was also a mason; Albert Else, 1849 and 1852. An early 20th century landlord was H. Hollingsworth.

I noticed recently, August 2000, that once again the decorators are working on the place - another name change - surely not!

The Cherry Tree Inn, Carterknowle Avenue

In c1900, there used to be a small farm and cottages surrounded by cherry trees on this site and I believe that a beer-house was opened there, probably in the farmhouse. At a later date, the cherry trees were cut down and only the stumps remained. When the buildings were demolished I don't know, but a new public house with the same name was built on or near this site in 1961. It was put up to provide for the adjacent Knab Farm Estate which was built during this period.

The Banner Cross Hotel, Ecclesall Road

The name Banner Cross comes, so I've been told, from an old Norse word "boena-kross," which means a cross of prayer. The cottage which was on the site before it became a pub, was inhabited by a cutlery worker who was a scale presser. It became a pub, a beer-house, in the 19th century. The pub which stands there today was built c1930.

I must be becoming quite well known now for attaching stories of interest to public houses by the thinnest and most tenuous of strings. Anyone who had ever heard one of my "talks" will back this up. So, here is another. It concerns the most famous, one might even say the most popular, murderer ever bred in Sheffield, Charles Peace. Many different versions, like the Spence Broughton story, abound about this little villain's life. This is my effort:-

He was born in Angel Court, just off Angel Street, on May 14th, 1832. This street took its name from the ancient coaching inn which once stood on the corner with Bank Street - it was destroyed by German bombing in December, 1940.

His father was a cobbler, but Peace spurned regular work from the very beginning, apart from odd short period, and he started his career as a pickpocket working usually either in the markets, or when it was in town, on the fairground which used to be just below where the Victoria Hotel stands today. In his spare time, he was a reasonable self taught violinist and pub singer.

As a villain he was soon attracting the attention of the local police, so perhaps he was a better entertainer than he was a criminal!

In 1851, aged 19, he was charged with house breaking, but acquitted; in 1854, he was sent down for four years for burglary and his chosen career was on its way! Released from prison in 1858, he married and moved to Manchester. Here, in partnership with another man, he burgled a house, was nicked and received six years penal servitude. This was the official way of saying imprisonment with hard labour. It seems that he didn't like hard work outside prison, so he was made to do it inside.

Not, it seems, a very successful criminal so far. In his short life of 32 years, by the time he was released from this stretch, he had served 10 years inside.

Back in Sheffield and reunited with his loving wife, he set up in business as a picture framer. For a while he flourished for he was clever with his hands. The business expanded and he moved to larger premises in West Street. It seemed a bad move, for the business then failed, so he gave it up and moved again, with his wife, to Manchester.

Not a lucky town for Charlie, for he was again convicted of burglary and this time he was sentenced to seven years penal servitude. As he probably served his time in the same prison, Strangeways, he had hardly been out long enough to lose touch with his convict friends.

When he was released on what in those days was known as a "Ticket of Leave", in August, 1872, now aged 40 years. He returned to Sheffield with his wife, an obviously very patient woman, and went to live in Orchard Street. Three years later, they moved to live in Britannia Road, off Main Road, Darnall. I don't know how he supported himself and his wife during this time, but I've got a pretty good idea.

Here in Darnall was where sex and its attendant problems raised its ugly head and he embarked on the course of action that was to lead him to the condemned cell and the hangman's rope!

Living close by in Britannia Road, were a married couple named Dyson. Peace was very much attracted to Mrs Dyson and began to make a nuisance of himself. When her husband found out, there was trouble, naturally enough, and after Peace had insulted Mrs Dyson, a case of spurned love perhaps, and assaulted her husband, the police took out a warrant for his arrest. When they arrived at his house, they were too late. Peace had done the sensible thing, considering his record, and done a runner. He'd left town.

This time he finished up in Hull, but after only three months, in the autumn of 1876, when he considered that the heat was off, he returned to Sheffield and resumed his pursuit of Mrs Dyson. The couple, perhaps to avoid Peace's unwelcome attentions, had moved house and were living in Banner Cross Terrace, Ecclesall. This would have been fairly rural in those days. (Here comes the pub connection!)

That November, 1876, Peace went out to Ecclesall and after very likely filling himself up with Dutch courage in the Banner Cross Inn (it became an hotel later), he went to the Dyson's house. Here different versions of this story disagree. One version says that Peace went into the house and, in front of his wife, shot Mr Dyson dead, then made his escape across the fields. I don't subscribe to that version. The one that I believe is that Mr Dyson walked into the house and found Peace and Mrs Dyson in what is usually referred to as a "compromising position". It seems to me that there must have been quite a lot of encouragement towards Peace from Mrs Dyson, otherwise surely he wouldn't have continued his pressing his attentions onto her? What happened then, I believe, was that there was a fight and getting the worst of it, Peace fled chased by Mr Dyson. In a passageway which led down the side of The Banner Cross Inn, Peace was possibly trapped, so he drew a revolver, turned and shot Mr Dyson and killed him. Then, he fled across the fields. The correct scenario, of course, could be neither of these versions, or a combination of parts of both. Anyway, Dyson was dead and Peace was on the run, wanted for murder.

Now seriously wanted by the police, he made his way back to Hull and maintained a very low profile. He knew, of course, the dreadful penalty for murder and knew that it was vital that he disguised himself. He shaved off his beard and dyed his hair, that was the easy part. What he really needed to hide was an injury that he had suffered in the past, some say the result of an accident in a steelworks, which had left him with two fingers missing on his left hand - enough to identify him to anyone. He got over this problem by making and wearing a false hand which slipped over his disfigured limb. The disguise was topped off with a pair of spectacles.

Perhaps the close proximity of Sheffield, the scene of his greatest crime, worried him, because soon he was on the move again. This time he headed towards London where he set up home.

It is very probable that for all this time he had been supporting himself and his long suffering wife through villainy and this he continued to do after he arrived in London. He was, it is believed, a very cunning and skilful burglar, although his early record tends to disprove this. Perhaps much practice, as in most things, made him better at it.

One night, however, while in the process of robbing a house in South London, he was challenged and then chased by a policeman. In his frantic efforts to escape, he shot the man dead. It seems that Peace habitually carried a firearm and wasn't afraid to use it.

He was, nevertheless, caught and when he was brought up in front of the magistrates bench at Greenwich Police Court, he gave his name as John Ward. The date was October 19th, 1878 and he was 46 years old. He had been on the run for almost two years. He was unlucky in that while on remand in Newgate Prison, he was recognised by a fellow prisoner who identified him to the prison staff, perhaps in the hope of currying favour. The game, or at least part of it, was up!

Peace came up for trial at the Old Bailey, the Central Criminal Court, on November 19th, 1878 charged with the wilful murder of a policeman while carrying out a felony. He was found guilty and sentenced to penal servitude for life. It is difficult to understand why he wasn't sentenced to death, for this was a crime that was hard to better. Perhaps he would have preferred it, for life at hard labour was a far tougher sentence than it is possible to hand down today. A "life" sentence in those days was far longer than it is now, and for killing a policeman, it would probably have meant what it said - for the rest of his natural life.

This was where the Sheffield police came onto the scene. They had been notified in the normal course of events about the trial and they realised that Peace was someone they wanted very much to interview. They applied for his transfer to Yorkshire and it was granted. It was on the rail journey up to Sheffield that Peace made his last, desperate bid for freedom. He leapt from the moving train, but injured himself and was recaptured.

Peace made his last public appearance at Leeds Assizes on January 24th, 1879. There, he was found guilty of the wilful murder of Mr Dyson. He was sentenced to hang.

Charles Peace was hanged at Armley Prison, Leeds on the morning of February 25th, 1879. One of his last recorded remarks concerned his breakfast - his last meal. "This is bloody rotten bacon", he said! I suppose that shows a certain amount of style!

The Rising Sun, Abbey Lane, Little Common

The landlord in 1786 was Samuel Brookshaw. The place at that time was a country beer-house. His is one of the four names included on the memorial stone to a wood collier named George Yardley, who burned himself to death in his cabin in Ecclesall Woods. The stone still stands today near to the site of the tragedy.

Mr Brookshaw was also a pocket and pen knife maker. In 1825 and 1841, the landlord was William Loukes. He was also a pocket knife and scythe maker. In 1845 and 1852, the landlord was James Ellis, also a woodman.

The days of this pub being a country beer-house have been gone many years, along with the countryside, and today, after another refurbishment, it is now an upmarket pub/restaurant, although basically the buildings are still the original ones.

The Barrel, Hoober Avenue / Ringinglow Road, Bents Green

This began as two cottages, although the exact location I don't know. In the trade directories of 1825 and 1841, the landlord is listed as Edward Loukes, who was also a butcher by trade. It is possible that he could have been related to William Loukes, landlord of The Rising Sun during the same period.

John Webster, a cutler and patten iron maker in Little Sheffield, kept a pub in Hermitage Street which had a bowling green. Patten irons, by the way, were fixed to wooden soles which were then attached to shoes to raise them above the level of the mud and garbage, which spread across both the roads and the footpaths in those days. They were much in demand.

There was an unknown pub at Broad Oaks which had a cockpit.

last orders

CHAPTER EIGHTEEN
THE WESTERN SUBURBS

When I began to put together this chapter. I ran straight into a problem - I couldn't think of a title. The problem was that the area it covers spreads a long way westwards and includes many hamlets and villages - Ranmoor, Fulwood, Crosspool, Lodge Moor, Sandygate and the Mayfield Valley plus Redmires Reservoirs and the Rivelin Dams. After that, it is all Derbyshire.

So, as I obviously didn't have a Grenoside or an Ecclesfield as a main chapter ingredient, a nice and compact village stuffed with pubs, I decided to ignore all the small centres of population and just give the chapter the general title of "The Western Suburbs". It seems to fit in pretty well.

I have studied maps, old and new, and I still don't honestly know where Ranmoor, Fulwood and the rest begin and end in relation to each other. It is, as I have said, a large area and over the years the old borders have blurred and been built over. I don't think that it matters too much. What does matter are the pubs and unfortunately this is not an area which supports too many. What pubs there are, though, are old and venerable; some support a fair amount of history.

This part of the Metropolitan District of Sheffield spreads out from the depths of prosperous suburbia to about as far as you can go before the houses disappear and the uplands begin. Here on the borders with Derbyshire it is high and windy, especially Lodge Moor. This place was often visited by relatives on their way to the rather grim, but necessary isolation hospital. This depressing collection of regimented buildings is, at the time of writing, closed and plans are afoot to create 44 flats in various existing buildings and to erect 189 houses on the rest of the site.

The countryside is dotted with isolated farmsteads and the pastures are sliced into neat geometrical portions by natural dry-stone walls. In the 13th century this was deer country and was known as the Forest of Riveling. Part of this glorious piece of Yorkshire is called The Mayfield Valley, a close knit community in years past, which has supported the same families for hundreds of years. Many of the old family names still crop up again and again.

One example is the Marsden family. I have picked this name, because this is primarily a book about pubs and this family did, in the 19th and 20th centuries, keep several pubs. I have already mentioned one Marsden in the previous chapter.

The ancient Anglo-Saxon name for Fulwood was Ful-Wudu. This meant a marshy woodland. It isn't like that now. The Victorian age of "in your face" prosperity was the cause for many of the large houses in Fulwood and Ranmoor and, to a lesser extent, other areas around here. The district has come a long way from when it was mostly deer-parks guarded jealously and reserved only for use by the serious gentry.

In the 17th century, there used to be a natural spring of water, allegedly rich in health giving minerals, which gave Fulwood the reputation of being a minor spa. This "spa" has long been either built over or has dried up and there are several theories as to where it used to gush healthily. One idea is that it was opposite Fulwood Old Chapel, Whiteley Lane. This Unitarian Chapel was built in 1729, is a beautiful old Yorkshire building and has, in its small front garden, an old set of stocks which could be the original Fulwood Village stocks. I mentioned them in the chapter on Ecclesfield.

The Three Merry Lads, Redmires Road

This public house, now owned by Joshua Tetley's, or whoever owns them now, has what must be a unique name and there are several stories about who exactly were these "Three Merry Lads"? This one, I believe, is the correct version:-

Luke Marsden, 1789-1861, the son of Richard Marsden, c1765-c1830, who lived at Bole Hill Farm on the corner of Blackbrook Road and Harrison's Lane, married Hannah Mallinson on January 14th, 1809 and together they produced a large family which consisted of six daughters and...three sons. These three boys were called Richard, the eldest, who was born in 1812; George, who was born in 1817 and the youngest, Benjamin, who was born in 1819. These made up the trio of "lads" which gave this beer-house its name.

They lived with their parents at a house in Redmires Road, called White Low, which had been built by their grandfather, Richard, for their father, Luke, on his marriage. This became, about 1832-1834, a licenced premises named by their father, after no doubt plenty of advice from his wife, Hannah, The Three Merry Lads.

It is probable that it became a beer-house to cater for the large number of navvies, who were working on the construction of the three Redmires reservoirs. These dams were completed in 1836, the upper dam; 1849, the middle dam and 1854, the lower dam. The length of time taken working on the dams would have assured any hostelry selling strong drink, in the near vicinity, at least 20 years of good customers (well, customers, anyway!).

I don't know when the pub received its full public house licence, but it was still a beer-house during the First World War. Like its neighbour, The Sportsman, which was another beer-house, it was popular with the troops who trained at Redmires Camp during the war.

Merry Lads grow up in time and here is a potted history of what they did with their lives:-

Richard, 1812-1868, the eldest of the lads, became a stone mason, bridge builder and for a time, a railway track foreman. Following his marriage to Elizabeth Parkinson, he lived with his wife and three daughters in the small cottage, possibly built by him, that still stands at the junction of Rivelin Valley Road and Manchester Road. This building is now, I believe, the Rivelin Post Office and is well known mainly for being at the end of the long walk along the River Rivelin which begins, if you want it to, at Malin Bridge. Richard Marsden was 56 when he died in 1868.

The second son, George, 1817-1884, married Charlotte Thorpe and they produced four sons and four daughters. The family lived at Crimicar Lane Farm. George, it is said, came to an unfortunate and tragic end due mostly to both a fondness for and an over indulgence of "the demon drink"!

On the night of January 3rd, 1884, he was making his unsteady way home from The Blacksmith's Arms, Willow Lane (now Fulwood Road), when he stumbled and fell into a horse trough which stood beside the edge of Crimicar Lane. This trough was fed by Crimicar Dyke, which ran nearby, and was always brim full. It was believed that he drowned partly because he was befuddled by drink and partly because of his habit of always walking with his hands in his pockets. This fatally hindered his efforts to escape from the watery embrace of the horse trough and led to his death by drowning. It's a story, anyway!

The youngest of The Three Merry Lads, Benjamin, lived at Fulwood Grange. I have noticed that many people think that any house that has "grange" in its name is, or was, somehow connected with the church - like priory or abbey. This is not so. It simply means a country house with farm buildings. He worked at Fulwood Grange Farm, which was owned by James Green.

Benjamin did what it has always been a smart thing for a young man to do - he married the boss's daughter, Mary How Green. They managed a huge and evenly balanced family of seven sons and seven daughters, all produced between the years of 1841 and 1863. Mary was only 47 years old when she died She was probably worn out!

The many sisters of The Three Merry Lads were well known in the district for the high quality smocks that they made for the local farmers and farm workers.

One sister, Sophia, the eight child of Luke and Hannah, never married and was only 32 years old when she died in 1857. She lived at home in the pub and behind it she ran a small "dame" school for the local farmers' children. These schools, privately run and financed by small charges, were capable of furnishing the children with an elementary education. This was probably all they ever received, or needed. Muriel Hall, the author of two fine books on the Mayfield Valley, tells about her great-grandfather, who used to visit The Three Merry Lads and while there, spend every penny that he had in his pocket. He would then sell his boots to buy more drink and have to walk to his home in Carr Road, a three mile journey, in his stockinged feet. That's dedication! He was born in 1812 and died at the age of 90 years old in 1902, so it couldn't have done him much harm.

The "Lads", as it is known locally, is now more of an eating house than a simple public house, in common with many pubs today, and is still a popular stopping off place along Redmires Road. The sign depicts three young boys playing. It is the latest of several interpretations which have appeared over the years and this time it seems as if the brewery have got it right.

The Grouse and Trout, Long Causeway, Redmires

The name of this now disappeared and once very isolated pub, built as it was on a high plateau, is redolent of the moorland on which it used to stand. There would have been plenty of grouse here, although I'm not sure about the trout. This account illustrates the large amount of power wielded by those who, by their wealth and position in society, considered it their right to exercise control over the moral welfare of those who they considered to be lesser mortals.

I don't know the exact date of when this pub was either built or when it became a pub. I do know

late 19th century

that, like others in the area, it was hugely popular with the navvies working on the construction of the Redmires group of dams. The pub was reputedly known by the navvies as "The Eyes and Ears". This was due to the fact that the strong drink they consumed in vast quantities caused many drunken fights and these resulted in much physical damage to each other.

Consider the life of a "navvy". These mostly itinerant, largely uneducated workers would have worked punishing hours, especially in the lighter summer months. Using only picks, shovels, wheelbarrows and muscle power they moved, literally, mountains of earth and rock to make the reservoirs. Accidents must have been normal; deaths commonplace. Life among these men was cheap. It is hardly surprising that this tough breed of men played as hard as they could, in the sparse free time that they were allowed, in the crude beer-houses that were all they could visit.

Living in rough shanty camps, or even rougher on the open moors, some were lucky enough to have the type of female camp follower that soldiers enjoyed during the Napoleonic Wars.

There were no home comforts, poor food, frequent outbreaks of disease and minimal contact with decent civilization. I have no statistics, but I wouldn't have thought the life span that they enjoyed, if that is the correct word to use, was very long.

At some stage during its life, the beer-house obtained a full public house licence, which was held until it closed in 1913. The reason for this closure was not due to any fault of the tenant at the time, Mr Taylor. The owner of the pub and also of the surrounding land was now William Wilson, of Beauchief Hall. I think that he was a member of the powerful Wilson snuff family. Mr Wilson was worried that, with the advent of the newfangled motor buses which had begun to reach out from Sheffield as far as Remires, the increasing numbers of the public travelling out to The Grouse and Trout and then trespassing on his moors would disturb the grouse and ruin his shooting pleasures. If the grouse were to stay, then the pub had to go - and so it went.

Before the last tenants, Mr and Mrs Taylor, took over the pub, it was kept for a number of years before the turn of the century by Mr and Mrs Gee, date unknown. Other 19th century landlords were Thomas Peacock, 1841, who was also a gamekeeper and George Green, 1849 and 1852.

The pub was demolished in c1950 and now all that it left of the pub buildings, which I believe were large and L-shaped, is the pub sign. I went on a pub sign hunting expedition one Sunday evening in the summer of 1999 and I was lucky enough to find it. It is a large, square block of granite, old and moss covered now, which still stands propped up against a stone wall beside what once was the entrance gate to the pub. On it is a rather worn stylised image of a grouse and below three trout. At the bottom, almost unreadable, is a motto, a play on the motto of the Prince of Wales - "Ich Dien Dinner"! It is nice to know that 19th century landlords had a sense of humour.

While chatting about this pub to a colleague, he told me the following interesting fact, it concerns his very elderly mother. Her name is Mrs Elizabeth Phelan neé White, she came from a local farming family and she was actually born on a table in the taproom of the Grouse and Trout. The date was 12th December, 1900 and this grand old lady will be 100 years old this coming Christmas!

There used to be a beer-house quite near to the Grouse and Trout which closed down in the 1880's. I'm not sure of its location, but a building is marked on an old map called Ocean View. This is just off Long Causeway and couldn't have been more than a quarter of a mile from the other pub. Again, it would have been opened to serve the dam workers. Why was it called Ocean View, which is, let's face it, a strange name for a building in the middle of moorland? Your guess is as good as mine. Was it to do with the large expanse of water which had suddenly appeared within sight of the building?

The Sportsman Inn, Redmires Road

This old pub stands very much alone on the opposite side of the road and marginally nearer to Sheffield than its neighbour, The Three Merry Lads. It also has a connection with the Marsden family.

Zenas Marsden, 1843-1900, was the second eldest child and eldest son of Benjamin Marsden. He was a large, thickset and rotund man, who spent part of his life working on local farms, part for the water company and part as the landlord of this pub. He farmed the handful of acres of land that went with it. He was not the first of Benjamin's offspring to run the pub. His sister, Clara, kept it with her husband when they were first married. She was married to Joseph William Dungworth, whose parents, I believe, kept The Lescar Hotel in Sharrow Vale Road. This pub is still open and is a popular jazz venue. This name, Lescar, is a corruption of the old words "leese carr" which meant a field with leeches. Gosh!

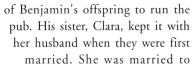

Zenas was married to Elizabeth Hudson, who died in childbirth while producing her 14th child. She was buried in Fulwood Churchyard in February, 1885. Her husband followed her there in February, 1900. Zenas sounds like a name with biblical connections, and he was indeed a dedicated churchgoer and also a fine fiddler. When, it is said, he was asked by the vicar of Fulwood, why he, a religious man, was contemplating taking over the running of a public house, he replied that if he didn't do it, then someone else would and anyway, didn't Jesus love publicans and sinners?

Following the death of Zenas in 1900, the pub was taken over by his eldest son, Arthur, 1866-1929, who had married Mary Ann Broomhead. She was a member of another large, local family. In 1915, the pub was the home of Mr and Mrs Taylor, who had moved from the now defunct Grouse and Trout not too far away. When that pub closed, Mr Taylor had hopes that when he moved to The Sportsman, which was a beer-house, he could obtain for it a full licence, the type he had enjoyed at The Grouse and Trout. It was not to be. When he put his application in front of the licencing magistrates, it was refused. The reason given by this august body of bigots seemed to be that as there was an Army training camp nearby, Remires Camp - the First World War had been underway for a year - which held about 1,000 men, it would be foolish in the extreme to put temptation in the way of "such men" by giving them the opportunity to purchase and drink "spirituous liquor". Beer was obviously good enough for ordinary soldiers! The officers, I have no doubt, were excluded from any such restriction and would have had a well stocked officers mess.

The Kings Head, Manchester Road

This detached, roadside public house is one about which I know very little. It has obviously been there for many years, at least as far back as c1830, and was bought by The Crowded Pub Company recently. About a year ago, someone from this Company telephoned my to ask if I could put together a short history of the pub. This was presumably to frame and display in the bar. They offered me money to do so, but with great regret I had to phone them back and tell them that, try as I might, and where money is concerned I try very hard, I could not discover anything historically interesting about the place. It was just an old, former coaching inn standing on what used to the Sheffield to Manchester turnpike. There were plenty of these.

Just before demolition

Since then the Crowded Pub Compay has moved out (obviously the pub was not getting crowded enough!) and the only really interesting event if the pub's history has been enacted - it was pulled down amid a storm of protest and after a short period of illegal occupation, from 25th May until its demise on 9th June, 2000, by a group of concerned "local residents and historians" - their own description.

The main problem, and one that the protestors couldn't overcome, was that the building didn't have any of the architectural qualities which would have given it listed building status. It was considered by English Heritage to be just a redundant old building and as such not worth saving.

Perhaps if this group of concerned local residents had, with their friends, spent a little more time and money in the pub it wouldn't have been sold off and the site redeveloped? Anyway, they got a good mention in the local newspaper, and the pub got demolished. Just before this book went to press, September 1st 2000, I read that the developers, McCarthy & Stone, have submitted a reduced planning application for the site which, if approved as has been recommended, will result in 32 flats plus car parking being constructed on the pub's site.

The Bell Hagg Inn, Manchester Road

Although I don't know when this became a pub, I think that the building was put up in c1832 by a man called Dr Hodgson. It was a five storey house built on the very edge of the escarpment and this gives it the superb view that it has across the Rivelin Valley. It was known for some years as Hodgson's Folly. It has very recently been refurbished and extended somewhat.

The strange name's possibly a corruption of Old English words, meaning warning beacon enclosure.

The Sportsman, Manchester Road / Benty Lane

This is another pub with little history that I can find. The building standing today is not too old, although there could well have been an older pub on the site at one time. Perhaps this pub's one claim to fame is that it was once kept by Ernest Blenkinsop, who was a legendary Sheffield Wednesday player in the pre-war years.

He also played over 20 times for his country.

The Crosspool Tavern, Manchester Road

Just down the road from The Sportsman, this pub began life as a cutlers cottage and a beer-house. In c1930, the site was cleared and the new public

house was built slightly to the rear. It is now one of Sheffield's best known pubs and has recently been extensively, but sympathetically refurbished. It is screened from the road by several mature trees which must date from the 1930's.

The Rising Sun, Fulwood Road, Nether Green

This is another pub, now in a heavily built up area of Fulwood, which has connections with the Marsden family - they are rather complicated. It was kept by William Marsden, 1883-1868, who was a son of Ruth Marsden, the eldest child of Luke and Hannah Marsden and a sister of The Three Merry Lads. She married a man with the same surname as herself, who came from Bradfield and thus didn't need to change her maiden name on her marriage. This is the sort of "quirk" that drives researches wild and rightly so. This made William a nephew of The Three Merry Lads.

William married Ann Creswick of Holmesfield and they had seven children. He died young, aged only 35 years old and was buried in Fulwood Churchyard.

The pub was a popular stopping off place for farm workers either going into Sheffield or returning. It was said that if anyone paid him with a note, then William, my genial host, would let them stay "supping" as long as they liked. However, if they proffered the exact money, then he would soon suggest that it was time they drank up and got back to their wives and families.

The pub was also a well known venue for the bull and bear baiting which took place there at various times of the year.

The Blacksmith's Arms, Willow Lane (Old Fulwood Road)

The description of this pub depends almost entirely on information that I gleaned by reading an article written by Colin Cooper, which is included in Muriel Hall's book, More of Mayfield Valley and Old Fulwood.

There once used to be a triangular piece of land just outside Fulwood village known as School Green. This was about one acre in area. Today it is still there and is bordered by Fulwood Road, Stumperlowe Lane and Stumperlowe Hall Road. The Blacksmith's Arms stood on the corner of Fulwood Road and Stumperlowe Lane and the group of buildings included a blacksmith's forge and smithy.

In the early 19th century, this piece of land, split into three fields and supporting only a barn, was acquired by one Christopher Oates, who also became owner of Stumperlowe Hall. Mr Oates sold the barn together with one of the fields to a local blacksmith called Farewell Harrison (Oh, my!)

By 1828, Mr Harrison had built himself a house beside the barn, turned the barn into his smithy and forge, taken out a beer-house licence and was described in trade directories as "a victualler, blacksmith and farrier of The Blacksmith's Arms, Goule Green". He was also a farmer in a small way, farming about 17 acres of local land. He was obviously making sure that he'd never go short!

In a trade directory of 1833, the pub was known as The Hammer and Pincers, but I think that this was either only a temporary name change, or the directory was wrong - it happens.

When Farewell Harrison died in c1845, his widowed daughter, Mary Swinden, took over the licence, but the blacksmiths business was bought by George Hodson from Todwick.

Over the years both blacksmiths and landlords came and went until c1863, when the property once more came back into the hands of the owner of Stumperlowe Hall. This was now Mr Henry Isaac Dixon. The days of The Blacksmith's Arms were numbered, however. During the late 19th century, roughly in the 1880's, the temperance movement was growing in popularity in some quarters, led by the various churches, and when for some reason, I don't know why, the pub was temporarily without a landlord, the Vicar of Fulwood, the Rev. JH Hewlett, persuaded the owner of the buildings, Mr Dixon, to surrender the licence and reopen the place as a coffee house. Mr Dixon agreed and the pub was closed for ever.

The coffee house flourished, however, supported no doubt by the spinster teetotallers of the parish, until 1936 when it was sold and became a private house. When I searched for the site of this old pub recently, I found that the whole of the triangle of land, once known as School Green, was covered in large, postwar, detached houses.

The Sun Inn, Shelborne Road / Cairns Road, off Manchester Road

This building was erected by Lord John Murray, but whether initially as a pub is not known. It had a datestone of 1774 and in 1798 it was described in a trade directory as "John Exley's Sign of the Sun".

There is a story about why it shut down. One night, a drunk was thrown out of the pub by the landlord, due to causing trouble, not for spending all his money, and it was believed that he must have hit his head or similar, because he died shortly afterwards. Although he was never accused of any crime, the landlord allowed the incident to prey on his mind to such an extent that he wasted away and on his deathbed he confessed to killing the man. This must have led to the licence being withdrawn.

The former pub buildings were used as a school for many years and was originally for delicate or convalescent children from the less healthy parts of the city. To be quite frank, I am not absolutely sure where it was, but the slim evidence that I have found leads me to believe it was just off Manchester Road.

The Plough Inn, Sandygate Road

This pub stands opposite to the football ground used by the Hallam Football Club. This football club is the second oldest in Sheffield, behind the Sheffield Club and one of the oldest in England. Their ground, I believe, is where the Hallam Chase begins and ends. This is a very old foot race which is run annually.

This is a large, detached public house, which dates back at least to 1825, although possibly not in the same building, when Richard Creswick was landlord. He was followed by Richard, his son, who ran the pub in 1841 and 1849.

Like most large pubs today, this house very much concentrates on the restaurant trade and seems to be popular.

The Bull's Head, Fulwood Road

Not much is known about this pub. It can be dated back as least as far as 1849 when the landlord was Jonathan Swann. It was once called The Highland Laddie and I can only think that this name was derived from the origins of one

of the landlords. Today it is a very well organised, tightly run and no doubt profitable suburban public house.

The Ranmoor Inn, Fulwood Road

This pub is very close to The Bull's Head and in many ways has faced the end of the 20th century in the same way. It dates from roughly the same date, c1852, when the landlord was James Worrall (or Worrell).

Carr Houses, Quiet Lane

This row of cottages are very much a part of the Mayfield Valley and, I believe, containted a beer-house known as Water Carr Hall in the late 16th or early 17th centuries. How long it was in business or who were the landlords or owners I have no idea.

The Shiny Sheff, Crimicar Lane, Lodge Moor

This pub was built in the late 1960's and first opened for business on April 22nd, 1969. The unique name commemorates the nickname given to the three Royal Naval ships which have borne this name. Shiny Sheff derives from the stainless steel fittings used on at least the first HMS Sheffield.

Commissioned as a cruiser, which is a warship smaller and faster than a battleship, but less heavily armoured, the first HMS Sheffield was very active in the Second World War and, in 1941, was part of the task force which chased the German battleship, Bismarck. This pride of the Nazi fleet was finally sent to the bottom on

May, 17th, 1941. Sheffield survived the war and when it was sent for scrap in 1957, the ship's bell, badge and flag were placed in the cathedral of St Peter's and St Paul's, Sheffield. The second ship given this name, a guided missile destroyer, was part of the British forces which were in the Falklands Conflict. It was the only major vessel lost when it was hit by a French made Exocet missile and burnt out on May 4/5th, 1982. There was great and tragic loss of life.

The present HMS Sheffield is a frigate, slightly smaller than a destroyer, which is still in service with the Royal Navy.

The pub is a shrine to the ships which have carried this name and the reunions of the ex-crew members of HMS Sheffield, whichever one of the three ships served on, are held in the pub.

Architecturally, it gives the impression that the idea was to make a pub in Sheffield which had the look of a Swiss chalet. If that was the idea, then it almost works.

There is a small, discreet stainless steel plaque in front of Sheffield Cathedral in memory of the men who have been killed in action while serving on HMS Sheffield.

I have heard these pubs mentioned, but I have no clear idea as to where they were situated:-

The Hole in the Wall, David Lane

This farm, which like so many others took out a beer licence to cash in on the influx of navvies working on the Redmires dams, stands at the top of David Lane. I know nothing more about it, other than that I think it took its name from a well known gate in a nearby natural stone wall.

The Bowl (or Pudding Bowl)

I believe that this was in Pitchford Lane, which was formerly known as Russell Lane. This name could have been a nickname.

The Hare and Hounds

This was probably where Sandygate Road joins Pitchford Lane.

The Ball, Sandygate

This vague address is about all that I know about this pub, apart from the fact that the landlady between 1841 and 1852 was Charlotte Wright.

last orders

CHAPTER NINETEEN
MOSBOROUGH VILLAGE

The name of this village is derived from Moreburgh which means "fort on the moor". Until 1967, when due to the anticipated need to accommodate the overspill from the ever expanding city of Sheffield, Mosborough and various other areas on the border between South Yorkshire and Derbyshire were absorbed into the city, this was a fairly small and self contained community which had, in years gone by, relied for its bread and butter on coal mining and such light industries as scythe and sickle making.

Today, it has steadily become a dormitory town which relies on Sheffield to provide work for a large number of its inhabitants. This wasn't an Act of God, it was planned. In the summer of 1966, the city council commissioned Clifford Culpin and Partners to prepare a "master plan" for the area. This was published in 1969 and contained, among other things, the proposal that by 1986, 15,700 houses should be built in what would then be known as the Mosborough Townships. There were to be 18 of these "townships", each supporting about 5,000 people together with backup facilities such as schools, pubs, shops and community centres.

As is usual in these matters, the plans were wildly off target and in fact the actual number of houses was reduced to 7,800, but then it was also realised that major retail outlets were required in the area. Thus, Crystal Peaks and Waterthorpe were created.

Many people who have lived a long time in the village and perhaps, like their parents, have been born there, bemoan, perhaps rightly, the ruination of Mosborough. All I can say is that this type of "progress" is happening all over the country. It must be a very short-sighted person who buys a house in a country village and who, thirty or forty years later, still expects the village to be as rural and Olde Worlde as when they moved there. As time moves on, populations increase and people need houses.

There have been a number of large, old houses in and around Mosborough over the years and I should like to mention two. Both these houses, once the homes of prosperous families, are now in various ways, part of the hotel industry.

Eckington Hall was built by Joseph Wells in 1871/2. Mr Wells was a member of a family of colliery owners who were, about this time, considered among the largest in England. His father, George, who died in 1844, had started the business and Joseph, in partnership with his brother, George, built up what they had inherited. Joseph was born in Eckington in 1816 and to honour the village of his birth, when he required to build himself a fine house, he wished it to stand in Eckington and he also wished to call it Eckington Hall. However, he was unable to find a suitable site in Eckington, so Eckington Hall was built in Mosborough nearby. Still, one wish out of two is not too bad! He had little time left in which to enjoy and gloat over his new home, however, as he died in 1873, aged 69 years old

Until recently, the hall was a popular venue for the then fashion of medieval banquets, but fashions change and at the time of writing this, 1999, the hall is closed and up for sale.

Mosborough Hall is probably the oldest existing building of any stature in the village. It is recorded historically as being there, in some form or another, as far back as the 14th century. It has housed a long list of Lords of the Manor with such exotic, Jane Austen names as Sir Robert de Stuterville; Sir John, Lord Darcy; Sir James Strangeways.... I won't carry on. After a while all this romantic history becomes a bore!

It is, however, worth mentioning that one owner of the hall, Joseph Stones, in the early 1700's, built a 100 foot long brew-house probably to supply the hall with its own beer. This wasn't actually a very unusual thing in those days, but perhaps the size of his brew-house was. Was he related to William Stones the Sheffield brewer? I wish I knew.

I have found several little stories about the village, I think that they are worth repeating:-

A man named Mr Gray bought a house in the village and employed two brothers, local men from Dent Lane, Edward and Joshua Littlewood, to alter and repair it. They had the reputation of being both good stonemasons and good scholars, although what being a "good scholar" means exactly I don't know.

While they were working on the building it was believed that, hidden in a secret place in a wall, they discovered a sum of money. This they kept. It wasn't known how large the sum of money was, but soon afterwards they lent £1,000 to a Sheffield lawyer, a Mr Greaves. This money they never received back, so perhaps some sort of poetic justice was at work here. This was between 1800 and 1825, so think of what that £1,000 would have been worth today!

At the beginning of the 19th century, there used to be a bull stake at the top of the small triangular piece of land known as Mosborough Green and bordered by High Street, Little Hill and part of Queen Street. These stakes were where, in those rather more barbaric days, bulls and sometimes bears were tethered to be tormented by dogs, while onlookers wagered on the result. A Mr Thomas Bolsover, who lived nearby kept both a bull and a bear for that purpose.

At around the same time, Mr George Bolsover, who was probably a relative of Thomas, kept a beer-house with a cockpit used for cock fighting. The local magistrate, Sir Sitwell Sitwell, who was a very influential member of the local gentry and who lived at Renishaw Hall, ordered that the cockpit should be done away with. Mr Bolsover refused and, such was the power of Sir Sitwell, in spite of his name, that the beer-house lost its licence. I wish that I knew the name of the place.

Sir Sitwell Sitwell was an ancestor of the famous Sitwell trio of poets and writers who lived after him at Renishaw Hall - Osbert, Edith and Sacheverell. Just how talented this sister and her two brothers were is difficult to gauge. I have a feeling that they were more famous for being famous than for anything else. There is a lot of that about these days!

In the early part of the 19th century, there were a number of beer-houses in the village which were nothing much more than the front room of a cottage. These were known as "jerry" houses. Whether they had a licence, or in those days even needed one, I don't know, but they were closed after 1850, when only "suitable" houses were allowed to stay in business.

One such a beer-house was kept by a man named Luke Staniforth. This seems to be a common Mosborough name. It crops up again and again in local history accounts, as does Bolsover, Rose, Rotherham and Keeton. During the celebrations in 1815, held in a field opposite the Duke William pub, to mark the British victory at Waterloo which signalled the end of the Napoleonic Wars, an effigy of the "baddy", Napoleon Bonaparte, was placed in a tree for the public to abuse. Luke became so overwhelmed either by patriotism or by strong drink that he broke his walking stick while thrashing the hapless dummy!

Another peace celebration happened in 1856, to mark the conclusion of the Crimean War. It was held in a field owned by the Earl Fitzwilliam. The people enjoyed themselves - the children were given breakfast, the women lunch and the men, those who were still sober enough to eat it, dinner. Entertainment was provided by horse and donkey racing, hunting the pig with the greasy tail (don't ask me!), climbing the greasy pole, fighting and being rude in the bushes - the usual old country pursuits.

This is a final paragraph that I have taken from a small book written by George Foster, "Reminiscences of Mosborough, 1886". It gives a very graphic picture of what village life used to be like. It could perhaps apply to many other villages as well:-

"During this period (1850-1886), Mosborough appears to me to have been emerging from something like a chrysalis state and transforming itself into a beautiful village. The wealthy people are beginning to notice its pleasant and salubrious situation. Some have already built beautiful mansions, whilst others have improved the old ones. Nearly all the old thatched cottages have been demolished, and lofty and comfortable cottages built in their stead. The little "jerry" houses of the last period have been done away with and only suitable houses are allowed a beer licence. The footpaths are no longer a single row of irregular and uneven paving stones, but are for the most part broad asphalted causeways with good curbstones. The chapels, shops and houses are no longer in semi-darkness within doors during eventide, with only a tallow candle of rushlight burning, but are illuminated by gas and paraffin, which is burnt in beautifully reflecting lamps. The people are no longer to be seen carrying water from the village wells, in cans and buckets with yokes and rims, in hot summers they sat for hours by day and night, waiting to be supplied by the insufficient trickling streams; but now they have water supplied to them in their houses. The sewerage no longer flows down the streets and gutters anywhere, offensive alike to sight and smell, but is conducted in proper underground channels. And now there is a grand cemetery for the parish, which is kept in good order, and in which the people take a sublime pleasure in cultivating the tops of the graves with flowers. This place is a vast improvement on the old churchyard at Eckington, where sheep are allowed - as they have been for years - to graze, and rub their greasy fleeces against the tombstones, and otherwise defile them, and some of the footpaths are in a wretched condition....."

During the period 1800 - 1825, all the pubs in Mosborough, there were four I believe, were beer-houses. If anyone required stronger drink, they had to travel to The White Hart at Eckington, which held a full public house licence. At this time, the landlord was Job Allen. He was followed as landlord by his brother, George. A nasty tale of the times tells of how the body of George's daughter, Ann, recently dead, was stolen from her newly made grave in Eckington churchyard by body snatchers.

I have divided the public houses in the village into two halves - those still open and those that have closed - they split about evenly. The ones still open, now of course all fully licenced, are first. I am indebted to both David English and Ray Dyson for their great help and for sharing their knowledge with me when I was searching out information about these places.

The George and Dragon, High Street

This was originally known as The St. George and Dragon and appears to be the oldest pub still in business in the village. It was there at least as early as the end of the 18th century. It brewed its own beer on the premises, as did several others I've no doubt.

The earliest landlord that I can put a name to was John Bolsover, who was followed by John Parr in 1833. Mr Parr planted the orchard that was destroyed to enable St. Mark's Church to be built in c1886; he was also a butcher. William Lund was landlord in 1841; James Booth in 1849 and George Plant in 1856.

The British Oak, Mosborough Moor

This pub has, as has the one before, a very old and popular English pub name. I have written elsewhere in this book about its derivation.

The buildings were erected in c1825, by a scythe and sickle maker called John Cowley. It was to be used as a private house. The contractor was Thomas White of Eckington. There is no firm evidence as to when it was first used as a public house, but it is probable that it was in the first half of the 19th century. In 1849 and 1856, the landlord was George Booth.

The Vine Tavern, School Street

The name of this pub probably comes from a vinery, which I have been told is still in existence at Vine Grove Farm, which is opposite the pub. The pub was built in c1880 by either Henry or Thomas Bargh of Eckington.

A local legend attached to this pub relates that Charles Peace, Sheffield's favourite murderer, used to frequent the pub and, as an accomplished pub singer and fiddle player, he used to entertain the tap room customers. As Peace committed his murder in 1876 and never afterwards lived in Sheffield, this means that either the pub was built rather earlier than I have been told, which is possible, or it was brand new when he used it, or it is not true. You choose!

Today it has been refurbished to form one large room

The Alma, South Street

This pub was there before 1850, but at that time it was a beer-house which brewed its own ale. What it was called then is not known, but when it became a fully licenced public house it took the name of The Alma. This name gives at least the earliest date that it could have been so called that, because the name derives from the Battle of the River Alma, which took place during the Crimean War. This pointless little war was fought during 1854/1855, between the Russians on one side and the British, French, Sardinians and Turks on the other. We won!

An extension was built about 1890 and this was made from local brick from J. Lee's Brickyard, School Lane. About 20 years ago, when repair work was being carried out on the gable end of the building, a large painted sign was uncovered which advertised Gilmour's Ales.

There used to be, it may still be there for all I know, an old glass widow pane in the tap room which had scratched on it WILLIAM STACEY 1879. What this means I'm not sure. It could just have been put there by a bored customer.

The Queen Hotel, High Street

Once known as The Queen's Hotel - subtle difference - this was built by a local shoemaker, Benjamin Rose in 1836, but whether it was immediately a pub or a private house I'm not sure. When it did become a pub it was first known as The Black Bull, which could well recall the bull stake that I mentioned earlier.

Today, the name is simply The Queen and although it is still the original building, the large, arched windows to be seen nowadays used to be, until well after the end of the Second World War, the doors to the pub stables, later put to use as barracks.

The Royal Oak, High Street

The name of this pub will have derived from roughly the same source as The British Oak, Mosborough Moor.

This was another public house which started life as a private house. In 1843, Robert Higginbotham Rose, a name like that deserves to be remembered, built what was to become the basis of the pub, as a residence for himself and his family. He was a joiner and wheelwright by trade and he died on July 30th, 1865, aged 55 years. The house was not converted to a beer-house until c1870.

Since the late 1940's there have been two lots of extensions and refurbishments carried out to the premises. The original cellars, which were built to lodge the wooden beer barrels of the time, were modernised to take the bulk beer tanks demanded by the fashions of the 1960's and 1970's. Fashions are always altering, however, not least in the pub business, and during the last go at altering the pub, these tanks were ripped out and the pub returned to keg beer.

In common with pubs in the good old days that have now gone, The Royal Oak supported a full range of teams based at the pub. One unusual indoor game, which is more common in the South of England, was "Ringing the Bull". This involved a metal ring, made of copper or the like and of about two inches in diameter. If it were possible, a genuine bull's nose ring was used. This ring was attached to a length of cord or stout string, the other end of which was secured to the ceiling. The object of the game was to swing the ring on the cord so that it caught onto a hook sunk either into the wall or into the back of the door. I have played this game in various pubs in Kent. It is a lot of fun and not nearly as easy as it sounds. It can cost you many pints of beer to learn the art!

The Wheel, Plumbley Hall Road

This pub is named after the colliery wheel which was part of the head-gear of the now abandoned Plumbley Colliery. I hope that the builders have done their homework regarding the foundations of this

pub, as beneath it there must be a honeycomb of old pit workings. Things are apt to subside if it goes wrong. This is a new public house which first opened its doors in 1962.

The Ridgeway Arms, Quarry Hill

Originally called The Crofts, it was first opened in a former large private house called Mosborough Hill House. For some reason that I have been unable to determine, it was later re-named The Ridgeway Arms. Obviously, there is some connection with the nearby village of Ridgeway. This is, because of its origins, a very large and imposing public house, although I might upset somebody by calling it so lowly a name.

The Joseph Glover, Westfield, Halfway

This was converted from a flour mill which for many years was owned and worked by the Glover family. When it first became a pub, about 30 years ago, it was called, very reasonably, The Mill. Inside there used to be a lot of pieces of the old milling machinery on display still in situ, but whether it is there today, I'm not sure.

These pubs have closed:-

The Fitzwilliam Arms, Mosborough Moor

This pub must have been named after the Earls Fitzwilliam. This once wealthy and powerful local family were the builders and owners of the white elephant known as Wentworth Woodhouse. This house, which is reputed to have the longest frontage of any private house in England, has changed hands twice in the last few years. The title, Earl Fitzwilliam, became extinct following the death of the 8th Earl. It was created in 1746. There have been two other pubs named after this family in Sheffield and four after their house. One of them is still open in Milford Street, Attercliffe.

The pub was opened in the late 18th century; it ceased to be a pub just before the Second World War and then it became either a private house or a farmhouse. The buildings on the site were demolished in the 1990's to allow for the construction of one of the many new housing estates which are now threatening to engulf the village. I have found the name of an early landlady, Maria Havenhand, who was in charge in 1849.

The Nag's Head, Halfway

This pub was generally known as The Halfway House, but whether this was an official name or merely a nickname I don't know.

It opened before 1800 and was owned until 1841 by Thomas Wolstenholme. He was a millwright and also owned Knowl Hill Mill. He also helped to restore, using his millwright skills no doubt, Park Mill, Eckington in 1826. The landlord in 1849 was Thomas Robinson, who was also by trade a cutler.

The pub was either rebuilt or extensively refurbished for the owners, Tennant's Brewery, in 1870. The contractor then was Miles Barber of Barlborough.

The pub buldings were demolished in the 1980's to make room for, as so often happens here, new housing and roads.

The Crown, Crown Corner

Crown Corner is the name given to the junction of High Street with Queen Street and Station Road, so even if the pub which once stood on this corner has gone, at least it can be still remembered through this name.

Built in the early 1800's, it was demolished in c1970. The large colliery owner, George Wells, used the tap room of the pub as a temporary office where either himself or his agent used to pay the wages to the workmen. This was a very common 18th and 19th century habit, which was finally stopped when it became quite obvious that it wasn't sensible, nor fair on his dependent family, to pay a bored, poor and thirsty workman his wages while actually still inside a public house. It is a practice which is still employed sometimes even today, especially in the building trade.

About this time, the pub was known as Becky Lee's. This was after the landlord's wife. His name was Thomas Lee. He built the pub and then left The St. George and Dragon to live there.

The landlord in 1849 was John Robinson. When he died in 1857, he was followed by his wife, Elizabeth. She was landlady for 28 years and was considered to be "clean and courteous". Wow! She died in 1884, aged 68 years.

The Sidney Tavern, Queen Street

I have sometimes seen this name spelt Sydney. This building was erected in c1825 as a private house by a sicklesmith named Robert Fields, He was quite well off and either bought or built houses in various places in the village. One row of cottages that he built became known as Smugglers Row - he had once worked in Liverpool as an excise man. Enough said, perhaps!

It was later converted into a public house, but once again became a private house in the 1950's, which is how it remains today.

The Duke William, Chapel Street

This was yet another pub which was sacrificed on the alter of Sheffield's expansion via the construction of new housing. The name is possibly something to do with William, Duke of Normandy. I mentioned him ealier in the book.

It was built in the late 1700's and was a beer brewing beer-house. In the early 19th century, it was owned by George Bolsover, who could have been the man that I mentioned earlier in the tale about the cock-pit. This couldn't have been the pub which lost its licence, so probably either this was a different man, perhaps the earlier George's son, or after losing his licence for one pub, he took another. All very puzzling.

In 1833, the landlord was George Fox; then in 1841, John William Sayles and in 1849, Ellis Park. It was enlarged in the 1860's and demolished in 1960's.

The Blue Bell, Chapel Street

Very near to The Duke William, this pub was built in the early 1800's and in common with its neighbour, it was demolished in the 1960's.

About 1825, a set of stocks was installed on a piece of vacant ground opposite this pub on Primrose Hill. It is believed that the only time they were used was once when a man came back from a christening at Eckington Church in "a drunk and disorderly condition".

The Butcher's Arms, Station Road

Around the turn of the last century is when this pub is thought to have been built. Whether it began as a fully licenced public house I don't know, but it was a beer-house in 1922, after which it became a private house. It was later used as a shop. During its time as a licenced premises, one room was used as a doctor's surgery.

The Brown Cow, High Street

This is one pub about which I know next to nothing. I know that it was situated very near to The Crown and that its name was very typical of the type of names found in a country village and one of the most popular. Strangely there have been several pubs of this name in the centre of Sheffield.

The Prince of Wales, Chapel Street

Again, this is a pub about which I know little. It was very close to both The Duke William and The Blue Bell, so it perhaps shared their fate. This group of three pubs would have made a nice little tour round for anyone who didn't want to walk too far. I know about the Prince of Wales, though.

The name probably refers to the Prince of Wales, who became King George IV. He was, to put it mildly, a well known libertine and rake and he gave his name, the Regency Period, to a part of British history well known for its loose living and self indulgence - at least for the monied, upper classes - the working classes just carried on working and being exploited, as usual. It was also, as a saving grace, a period of great artistic appreciation which was led by the future George IV

He was known to his intimates as Prinny (or Prinney) and there are still pubs today with that name. When he became Prince Regent, due to the bouts of madness suffered by his father, King George III, there were pubs so named. There were, of course, pubs named The George IV. One of these is still open in Sheffield.

He was born in 1762 and died in 1830 having reigned for 10 years.

If the pub was built a long time later, then the Prince of Wales commemorated on the sign could possibly have been the future King Edward VII. He was another German bred royal, who enjoyed life to the full. He was born in 1841, the second child of Queen Victoria, in whose shadow he lived until she died in 1901. He reigned for nine years and died in 1910. He left behind a period in British history known as the Edwardian age.

Two pubs about which I know very little are The Grapes, Mosborough Moor, whose landlord in 1833 and 1841 was James Rowbotham; and The New Inn, which was kept by Thomas Lee in 1833 and 1841. Was he the same man who used to keep The Crown, Crown Corner?

CHAPTER TWENTY
BEIGHTON AND HACKENTHORPE

This area of South Yorkshire is no sparsely populated moorland waste; neither is it a picturesque landscape worthy of praise and adulation. There is plenty of history here though. This shows that at the time of the Norman conquest, and before that in Saxon times, there have been settlements; there have been farmers. In those early days, the farming of crops was done by the "strip" system. There were also plentiful woodlands to supply the important timber, which was then what man-made materials are to us today. .

Records exist today, which show that in the Tudor period there was a cutlery industry here, although it can be considered to have been in its fairly crude infancy. This was supported by power from the waterwheels along the Shirebrook valley. There was also coal mining, although evidence seems to suggest that this industry was being practiced earlier than Tudor times. In 1347, an inquest was held to investigate the death of one Hugh Wadshelf, a common shepherd, who while searching for lost animals, as shepherds do, fell into a disused coalpit and was drowned. This seems to indicate that the pit was not too deep. I believe they were called bell pits. The coroner's jury ordered the pit to be filled in.

In the 1950's, when the whole country plunged into a building boom, as a reaction against the recently ended Second World War, large housing developments were started in the Beighton and Hackenthorpe areas and since then much of the former peaceful rural ambience has disappeared. Nobody should have been surprised at this, after all, large housing developments and rural peace can never mix.

Up to April 1st, 1967, Beighton Parish was still part of Derbyshire, but after a sometimes bitter fight between the "for" and "against" factions and a discussion in Parliament, Sheffield finally won the day and Beighton Parish became part of South Yorkshire and the City of Sheffield.

As a rough guide to just how much Beighton has grown in the last 160 years, the following figures are of some help. They are, of course, only population figures and don't give much indication about how the infrastructure of the parish has altered. In 1801, the population of Beighton was 634; in 1961, this figure had risen to 23,056. These figures are now almost 40 years old and the population will have increased a great deal since 1961.

During the reign of Queen Elizabeth I in 1577, a survey of Beighton was made. This listed five "ale-houses" in the village. These were kept by George Hobson, John Teilour (Taylor?), Nicholas Young, Raffle (Ralf?) Lee and William Rawlinson.

Today, there are three active public houses in the village. There used, until fairly recently, to be a fourth, but The Railway Inn closed down in the 1950's. All the existing pubs date from the 19th century, if not earlier. The landlords named in this chapter do not always follow one another exactly, there are gaps in the dates.

The George and Dragon, High Street

The first pub of the three which have been on this site, was erected in 1780, was a beer-house until c1910 and was initially called The Kingston Arms. This was possibly after the Dukes of Kingston upon Hull. There were only two of these

dukes and the title only lasted from 1715 to 1773, when the second and last duke died. The name was changed in 1800 to The George and Dragon. It was often referred to as "The Low Drop" by the locals.

William Watts was landlord in 1827, he was also by trade a blacksmith so there was probably a smithy beside the pub. The following is a list of incumbents since that date:-

Hannah Watts, possibly William's widow, 1849; George Scholfield, 1857-1861; Edward Turton, 1871-1895; Henry (Harry) Hutton, 1908-1909; Williamson Glover, 1910-1930; Mary Glover, again possibly his widow, 1935-1940; Leonard Ansell, 1944-1954; Frank Johnson, 1954-1959; John Weaver, 1959-1965; Phillip Mulvaney, 1965-1969 - during his tenure, the pub, to all intents and purposes, was entirely rebuilt - Stanley Bonsall, 1969-1971 and Laurence Walker, who took over in 1972. There have been several other landlords since then.

The Royal Oak, High Street

Early in this pub's life it was known simply as The Oak. The first trio of landlords were all members of the Crookes family, although their exact relationship is not known. This family ran the pub between the years 1841 and 1895 and were John, also a wheelwright and joiner; William and finally, Charles Crookes. These were followed by George Banks, 1908-1914; Arthur Cutts, 1920; Frank Rogers, 1925-1927; Agnes Taylor, 1928; Charles Holden,

1929-1930; Henry Morris, 1935; Charles Stevenson, 1940; William, then Mrs Widdison, 1944-1954; Frederick Ball, 1956-1965; William Turner from 1967, then Christopher Piece.

This pub is involved, although only slightly, in the story of the building by the Manchester, Sheffield and Lincolnshire Railway Company of a new railway line between Woodhouse Junction and Gainsborough. This had to pass over a viaduct, which was to be built near to Beighton. This construction passed over the River Rother and during its erection, there was a prolonged period of very heavy rain, which swelled the river to flood level.

The contractors were under huge pressure to complete work on the viaduct before winter set in. The reason was commercial, I suppose, it being bad for business to have a railway standing idle. Whether construction mistakes were made through rushing the work, or whether it was simply that the weight of the flood water and debris forcing against the newly built structure was too much, is not known, nor does it now matter.

What matters is that the viaduct collapsed on September 30th, 1848. Onlookers said that it was like watching a huge row of dominos tumble down!

Not much time was wasted in recriminatuions and work began immediately to rebuild the ruin. Working throughout the winter in what must have been cruel conditions, the arches finally stood completed and the last keystone was knocked into place on the final arch on April 17th, 1849.

That evening, Mr RT Carlisle, the building contractor, who was no doubt a mightily relieved man now that the job was finished, took the entire workforce plus their friends, some 160 people, to dinner at The Royal Oak Inn.

I said at the beginning of this story that the pub was only slightly involved, didn't I? I still think that the tale was worth the telling.

The Cumberland Head, High Street

Up until c1895, this pub was a beer-house. Today it is fully licenced and merely known as The Cumberland. I don't know why. Many pubs have nowadays had "inn" or "tavern" tacked onto their names, completely meaninglessly - this one lost its head!

The name probably comes from the Duke of Cumberland who, in 1746, defeated the Jacobites under Prince Charles Edward (aka Bonnie Prince Charlie) at the Battle of Culloden.

This man was known throughout Scotland, at

least, as Butcher Cumberland and was widely hated for his actions following this battle which was bloody enough on its own. He ordered his English troops to pursue the fleeing Scots and to not only destroy them, but to destroy their wives, children, any other relations that they found and to burn all property they came across. In some isolated glens of Scotland, this barbaric man and his needless cruelty are still remembered with hatred.

This is the third pub on the High Street and again, it is traceable back to the beginning of the 19th century and maybe even further.

In 1846-1857, Thomas Turton was landlord, he was also a butcher by trade. He was followed by:- Alfred Hydes, 1859; William Crookes, 1861. Was he the man whom I mentioned earlier as a landlord of The Royal Oak, I wonder? Then William Cooper, 1868-1872; John Mirfin, 1879-1881; F. Morley, 1885; George Valentine Bower, 1895; William John, 1908-1910. He was followed by his probable widow, Rose John, 1914-1940; Ivy Lowe, 1944-1948; Herbert Lowe, 1951. Was he a relative, I wonder, of Mrs Lowe - a son, perhaps? Reginald Levick, 1953-1963; Arthur Allcock, 1963-1972 and Mr Siddall, who came from The Halfway House Hotel when it was demolished. Now a free house, it has been extensively modernised and its small frontage belies its large interior.

The Railway Hotel

This pub was next to the old railway station, which was built when the North Midland Railway ran a line through the village in May, 1840. This was, however, a fairly short lived enterprise for it closed down three years later in January, 1843.

When the more successful Manchester, Sheffield and Lincolnshire Railway started their railway line at what was to become Beighton's long standing railway station, The Railway Inn finished up standing a long way away from anything much to do with railways. This didn't affect it too much, because it stayed in business for over 100 years before the licence was transferred to a new pub, The Fox Inn, which was built in the 1950's in Robin Lane. The old pub buildings went the way for most old buildings and were knocked down.

When the pub was in business, because of its close proximity to the River Rother, it was prone to flooding as soon as any decent amount of water entered the river.

The pub was supplied, at least for some period of its life, with beer from Mappin's Old Brewery, Greasbrough Road, Masbrough, near Rotherham. This was a brewery begun by that well known and prolific benefactor of Sheffield, John Newton Mappin, 1800-1883, who I have mentioned in an earlier chapter.

Although I don't know the name of whoever ran the pub during the short time that it was a real "railway" pub, I can start shortly afterwards in 1846, when Thomas Murfin was landlord. He was there until 1859 and he was followed by:- William Boaler, 1861; Ann Boaler, 1868-1884, his widow; Henry Boaler, 1895-1909, possibly their son; William Wells, 1910; John Wilson, 1914-1920; Henry Morris, 1921-1930; This appears to be the same Mr Morris, who was landlord of The Royal Oak in 1935; R Wright, 1935-1940; Mary Wright, 1944-1948; Mary Widdowson, 1951. The man who had the dubious honour of putting the towels over the pumps for the final time was Mr Rylett, who then left to take over

The Fox, Robin Lane in 1955.

This smart modern pub will, I have no doubt, eventually gather some atmosphere and history, but it hasn't yet.

These above pubs weren't the only licenced premises in the village, there are two more, both clubs:-

The Beighton Miners Welfare Club, High Street

Before becoming a working mens' club, the buildings were first occupied by a farmer. Then they became attached to a golf club, before being bought in 1927 by the Miners Welfare Organisation for £3,104; the site covered about eight acres.

It was run, as most working mens' clubs were in those days, with a strict "men only" slant. Women were not even allowed to enter the premises, let alone take part in its activities. This ban was not lifted until 1943.

The club thrived and in 1973, larger premises were built on the site, although shrewdly the original club buildings were not demolished, but rented out as a dance centre.

Beighton Social Club, Manvers Road

Formerly a scouts meeting hall, then The Mayfair Dance Hall in 1936, this club used to be known as The British Legion Club. In 1957, it changed its name to The Queen's Road Social Club until it became known by the name it uses today.

In Hackenthorpe, there are more new pubs than old ones. This is not too surprising really considering the large amount of new housing, which has flooded over this part of the former Derbyshire countryside since just after the Second World War.

The Blue Bell Inn, Main Road

This is now known simply as The Blue Bell and has only been a fully licenced public house since 1949. Before this date it was a small, single roomed beer-house for over 100 years.

In 1833, it was run by James Staniforth and his successors were, unfortunately without dates, Elizabeth Linley; John Rowbotham; Sarah Brown; Mr or Mrs Woughingham; Joseph Binney; William Lanacre; Thomas Atkin; John Henry Frith; Eliza Frith, possibly John Henry's widow; Ernest Barber; Mr Barber was in charge of the pub until it was refurbished and extended in 1955.

At this time the pub was owned by the Richdale Brewery Company, Britannia Brewery, Bramall Lane, Sheffield. This brewery was established in 1860 and, until 1894, it traded as Richdale and Tomlinson Ltd. It was registered as Richdale's Britannia Brewery Co. Ltd. in 1898 and was taken over by Hammond's Brewery of Bradford and Rotherham in 1956. Shortly afterwards, Richdale's name disappeared. When it was taken over, this middle sized Sheffield brewery owned 25 tied houses and had a large free trade supply business.

The New Inn, Sheffield Road

The premises which used to be inhabited by this public house are now a veterinary surgeon's practice, known as New Court. This happened in 1959, when the pub's licence was transferred to the newly built pub, The Golden Plover, which had been recently completed in Birley View Road.

Before 1910, the pub was a free house owned by Thomas Staniforth. It was a well setup pub with extensive outbuildings and stabling next to the main block.

Starting in 1833, the following list of landlords and landladies are again without dates:- Martha Booth; James Staniforth, a possible relative of Thomas; George Staniforth, again a possible relative; William Nelson, who was always known as "Dandy" due to his fondness for wearing fancy waistcoats; Matthew Helliwell; Betsy Helliwell and Harry Helliwell. These three would, no doubt, have had some family relationship, husband, then widow, then son seems reasonable, although I have no proof of this. For some years, the pub was nicknamed "Betsy's" so Mrs Helliwell must have left her mark on both the customers and the pub!

This was during the time that the pub was tied to The Hope and Anchor Brewery Ltd. This pinpoints the time that Betsy ran the pub as being after 1942, because this was when The Hope and Anchor Brewery was formed following an amalgamation of the Henry Tomlinson's Anchor Brewery Ltd, Cherry Street, off Bramall Lane,

Sheffield with Carter, Milner and Bird's Hope Brewery, Claywheels Lane, Sheffield. This had moved from its Mowbray Street premises in 1938. Tomlinson's Brewery was damaged by enemy bombing in 1940. The Ship Inn, Shalesmoor is a rare pub which still has Tomlinson's name across the front of the building

The Hope and Anchor Brewery was taken over in 1954 by Truswell's Brewery, Eyre Street when it owned 240 public houses.

The Sportsman Inn, Main Street

From at least as far back as 1833, this was a free-house pub until the death of the landlord of the time, John Henry Frith in 1910. His widow, Caroline, took over as a tenant running the business for the owner, Walter Booth.

Mr Booth contracted with SH Ward's Sheaf Brewery, Ecclesall Road, Sheffield for them to take over the pub for a period of five years. After this period had expired, the ownership of the pub passed to The Old Albion Brewery Co. Ltd, Ecclesall Road, Sheffield. They owned it until c1950, although by that time the brewery had been absorbed, in 1939, by The Worksop and Retford Brewery Co. Ltd.

Following the change of ownership of The Old Albion Brewery together with the planned development of much new housing in Hackenthorpe, it was decided to knock down the original pub and build a larger and much more up to date replacement on a new site some way behind the site of the old pub. This happened some time towards the end of the 1950's.

A list of the landlords from 1841 is as follows:- John Booth; John Booth Jr, the earlier John's son; John Bramall; Joshua Binney; Walter Booth; John Henry Frith, already mentioned as a landlord of The Blue Bell Inn, Main Road; Charles Rippon; Tom Lancaster, who was well known for always smoking cigars; Harry Lancaster; Winifred Lancaster - there seems to have been some relationship between these last three names; William Watson.

The following pub used to be in Birley Spa, which is to all intents and purposes a suburb of Hackenthorpe. In the 19th century, the spa bath was very popular due to the supposed health restoring properties of its spring water. It is still standing and, although I believe plans are afoot by Sheffield City Council to restore it and make it once more amenable, to a large extent it has for many years been ignored by the public.

The Bath Hotel, Birley Spa

The mineral spa now known as Birley Spa, and which is Grade II listed, was built in 1842 by the Earl Manvers of Thoresby Park, near Worksop. It is South Yorkshire's only surviving Victorian bath house. I don't think that there were very many to begin with! The public house was built as an integral part of the complex.

Earl Manvers was a member of the Pierrepont family, who were the short lived

Dukes of Kingston upon Hull. The Pierreponts' were also descended from the legendary Bess of Hardwick of Hardwick Hall. She was a much married and extremely shrewd lady. The Earl Manvers title is also extinct and the house in Thoresby Park has for many years stood empty and forlorn, the contents sold. I have been told that it is in the process of being converted into a large, 212 bedroomed country hotel - the fate of a huge number of former stately houses, but infinitely better than them being knocked down. It is owned now by Warner Holidays and is a Grade I listed building, so care must be taken. There is, so I believe, a colony of bats, who live in the roof space, and there is to be a special enclosed area put aside for this protected species.

The original Victorian spa complex, which has been slowly deteriorating for years, has been promised, at the time of writing this, a large amount of money from various sources. This money is earmarked for renovation works. By the time you read this book, this may or may not have happened.

Working from 1845, the tenants or managers of the pub were:- George Eadon; John Tillotson; William Budd; Alfred Lee; John Bradley and the probable final "gaffer" in 1878, Thomas Lomas. It was after this date that the Birley Spa Baths began to fade in popularity and likewise the number of customers using the pub. It was then closed down.

When the new council housing estate in Hackenthorpe was built, apart from the previously mentioned Golden Plover, another pub was built in Delves Road. This was called The Hogshead. There is a Hogshead in Orchard Square in Sheffield. This is the third name given to the former Museum Hotel in the last ten years, since it was re-opened following complete rebuilding of the original pub, save for its listed facade. Whitbread's own a chain of about 150 public houses up and down the country all called "The Hogshead", although I believe that recently the company sold its public houses to concentrate on other business areas.

CHAPTER TWENTY ONE
WOODHOUSE

This was once a large, old and attractive village which, from at least the middle of the 19th century until the latter half of the 20th century, relied heavily for male employment on the ring of coal mines which surrounded it.

Today, the pits have gone and most of the old village buildings have been sacrificed to allow for progress and redevelopment and, although larger than it has ever been, the village has changed even within living memory.

Probably the oldest still inhabited building that is now left in the village is the former Old Cross Daggers Inn. This stands in the Market Place and together with the ancient market cross, which has recently been partially renewed, and the village stocks, forms all that is left of the historic centre of Woodhouse.

Of the old buildings remaining, the two main groups are the churches and chapels and, of course and thank goodness, the public houses.

During the Victorian era, there was a tradition of fruit growing in the area around the village and there were a number of orchards. These are now gone.

The village derives its name from the Old English "Wodehus", meaning "a house in a wood" - but then you had already worked that out, hadn't you?

The Old Cross Daggers, Market Place

If the datestone of 1658 above the door is correct, then this is a very old building indeed, and until it became a restaurant, it was probably one of the oldest remaining public houses in South Yorkshire.

It is believed that the building was built by a local landowner and staunch Quaker, Thomas Godfrey Newbould and the letters NTG beside the datestone are probably to do with him or his family.

Initially, like so many pubs in those days, it would have been a beer-house with its own brewing facilities. It was bought by the Sheffield brewers, Rawsons, and then, in the 1940's, it merged with the Joshua Tetley organisation. In the days before the village had its own post office, the pub was the collection point for all the local letters.

The Staniforth family, well

The Old Cross Daggers and the village stocks c1999

known publicans all over this area, held the licence for over 150 years and the family name appears in the histories of both The Angel Inn and The George Inn, as well as others.

In 1833, the landlady was Mary Staniforth. She was followed by John, in 1841, then Robert between 1856 and 1868. The last member of the family, Mrs Redfearn, finally relinquished control of the pub in 1958, when Frederick Hobson took over the reins. Until its conversion to a restaurant in c1969, it was run by JJ Meadows.

The Royal Hotel, Market Place

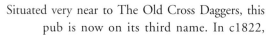

Situated very near to The Old Cross Daggers, this pub is now on its third name. In c1822, when the landlord was William Champion, it was known as The Bull's Head. By 1851, both the landlord and the pub's name had changed - to Joseph Taylor and The Coach and Horses. This name and Mr Taylor lasted about 10 years and then the final name, The Royal Hotel, appeared with Thomas Garner as landlord. I don't know if the name changes were the choices of the landlords, but if this was the case, then this is the first time that I have ever heard of this happening. I'm not sure when the present building was erected, but it seems to be a 1930's mock tudor style.

The Angel Inn, Chapel Street then Sheffield Road

This is another pub with a rather strange history. I have dated it back to at least as early as 1800, when the landlord was T. Widdowson. At that time, until 1862, it was called The Bull. This was perhaps because of the bull-baiting which in those days took place on the nearby village green.

When this "sport" was outlawed, it could have been the reason that the pub changed its name to the more gentle, Angel. James Littlewood was the landlord in 1841 and 1864, followed by William Staniforth, 1864 and 1868.

The old pub was demolished in 1925, for road widening. All, however, was not lost. The pub moved to Prospect House, a large, detached former private house in Sheffield Road. The first landlord after the pub reopened in its new location was Ernest Dyson.

The Angel has had several brewery owners:-

The Hope and Anchor Brewery; Truswell's Brewery; Joshua Tetley's Brewery and William Stones Brewery. In which order, though, I'm not at all sure. It is now in a relatively new building.

The Queen's Head

I don't have much information about this pub, not even its location. All I do know is that the landlord in the mid-19th century was Henry Hawksworth.

The Normanton Springs, Normanton Spring Road

This pub is still open, but I have no history about it.

The Stag Inn, Market Place

This building dates back to c1721, according to a datestone on the front of the building. Then it was a private house owned by a flour miller and baker called Samuel Atkin. The landlord from 1885 until 1909 was John William Cook.

He was a well known local bandmaster and fronted the Woodhouse Prize Band for many years.

Some modern landlords have been:- George and Joyce Woodhouse from 1964 until 1982, then James McGuigan until 1991. The pub was enlarged in 1909 and market stalls were often set up in front of it.

The George Inn, Market Street

The first use of this building was as a farmhouse after it was built by a Mr Birls sometime in the early 19th century. Today, the pub has been heavily modernised. The first recorded landlord, after it became a beer-house, was John Staniforth in 1856. Two other 19th century landlords were John Cartledge and Matthew Ellis. In 1905, Albert Bird was in charge and he was followed by John Wheatley, Stephen Waterhouse, Jabez Cox, Ronald Morley, Percy Smith, Ronald Pugsley, Percy and Ada Bower and Michael Attwood.

The Brunswick Hotel, Tilford Road

All I know about this pub is that it was once kept by the former Sheffield United footballer, Albert Cox.

There used to be another Brunswick in Haymarket, Sheffield, but it closed in the 1970's. The name, I think, may come from the family name of the wife of King George IV. He married Caroline Amelia Elizabeth, the daughter of Charles William Ferdinand, The Duke of Brunswick-Wolfenbuttel. Their marriage was, even by today's standards, scandalous. She was an immensely fat woman with mucky habits, who preferred to live on the Continent with her young lover and, when she arrived back in England to attend her husband's coronation, he ordered that she should be shut out of Westminster Abbey and excluded from all the celebrations. The public loved it!

The Junction Hotel, Station Road

This pub used to be owned by Rawson's Brewery, Pond Street, Sheffield. They were bombed in the war and the remains of the brewery and its pubs were taken over by Duncan Gilmour's Brewery. Gilmour's themselves were absorbed by Joshua Tetley's Brewery and thus the pub changed hands several times.

In the 19th century in 1856, William Ellis was landlord; in 1862 and 1864, Robert

Hepplestone, who was also a coal owner; in 1868, James Dabell. From 1907 until 1917, the landlord was Robert Pashley and from 1923 until 1961, John Dale Ellis was in command for 38 years - a fair innings!

The Working Mens' Central Club, Beighton Road

This used to be known as The Lambcroft.

The Princess Royal, Retford Road, Woodhouse Mill

Not strictly in Woodhouse village, this is a large, detached pub which is almost on the site of a former public house. It dates back to the middle of the 19th century and was possibly named after Princess Victoria. She was the eldest daughter of Queen Victoria and married the Emperor of Germany. Her son, Wilhelm II, was better known during the First World War as "Kaiser Bill".

The landlord in 1856 was Thomas Wostenholm followed in 1862-1868 by John Wortley.

There was a pub called The Greyhound in Woodhouse somewhere, but no-one seems to know where it was. All I know is that the landlord between 1864 and 1868 was John Ellis.

IN CONCLUSION.....

After a great deal of research and some thought, I have come to the conclusion that Sheffield and its surrounding garland of villages have lost just about all the pubs that are going to be lost. To put it bluntly, the ones which couldn't shape up have shipped out. I read recently that seven pubs a week are closing in villages throughout the country. That, by any standards, is an awful lot of pubs! I cringe everytime I hear about one closing in our area, but what alternatve is there. If the customers won't come, the money in the till doesn't pay the overheads......

This can only be to the benefit of the beleaguered customers, and let us face it, that is exactly what we are. If a pint of milk had gone up by the same percentage that a pint of beer has gone up in the last twenty years, there would have been riots in the streets years ago.

There will no doubt be a few more that close over the next few years, but the ones that have survived will have realised just that - they have survived, they haven't been given a meal ticket for ever - and it will only be by their efforts that they remain that way. Less pubs will make the breweries or whoever owns the place try harder to offer more, to keep prices down and to value their customers more. The only real tragedies caused by the closure of village pubs is when it was the only one in the village. But perhaps when that happens, the villagers should examine why it did close. They will probably discover that it was because they didn't ever use it, except to get drunk at the New Year.

I'm glad that the Great British Pub has developed the way it has. I spent my formative years in pubs that were grubby, chilly and hidebound by archaic licencing laws; they served warm beer of sometimes doubtful quality and the only food usually available was either a pickled egg, a packet of peanuts or a bag of crisps. I met many "genial hosts" whose sole aim in life seemed to get me outside onto the pavement on the stroke of closing time. It doesn't happen now, not if the pub wants to stay in business.

If you have got this far, then that means that either you have cheated or you have waded through my book. I thank you for that, I hope that you gleaned some information from it and some entertainment.

FURTHER READING

1 Drawings of Historic Totley by Brian Edwards
2 Totley & The Tunnel by Brian Edwards
3 Dore, Totley & Beyond by Brian Edwards
4 The Old Days In Dore edited by Roy Bullen
5 The Sheffield Way by Peter Price
6 Anston: Then and Now - Volumes One & Two
   by Bob Gellatly & Pem Stratford
7 History of Langsett and A Few More Stocksbridge Stirrings by Jack Branston
8 Walks Around Stocksbridge compiled by South Yorkshire County Council
9 Around Stocksbridge by Stocksbridge & District Historical Society
10 Around Stocksbridge: The 2nd Selection
   by Stocksbridge & District Historical Society
11 Sheffield Curiosities by Duncan & Trevor Smith
12 A Pub On Every Corner by Douglas Lamb
13 Lest We Forget by Douglas Lamb
14 Central Sheffield compiled by Martin Olive
15 Mottershaw's Sheffield by Pauline Shearstone
16 Stannington in 1851 by NE Reaney
17 Ecclesall compiled by Ecclesall Local History Society
18 How They Lived in Old Ecclesall by Mary M Bramhill
19 Sheffield's Remarkable Houses by Roger Redfern
20 Listed Buildings in Sheffield by English Heritage
21 A New General & Commercial Directory of Sheffield & Its Vicinity
   by R Gell (1825)
22 Fine Old Sheffield - An Historical Walk With Henry Tatton edited
   by Sylvia Anginotti
23 Grenoside, A Brief Historical Survey by Chris Morley
24 Glimpses of High Green's Past edited by JL Jones
25 High Green in the 1920's by Stanley Ellam
26 Chapeltown & High Green by Joan & Mel Jones
27 Old Chapeltown by MA Thompson
28 Sheffield in the 1930's by Peter Harvey
29 A Second Helping of Peter Harvey's Sheffield
30 A Third Helping of Peter Harvey's Sheffield
31 The Great Sheffield Flood 1864 by EG Draper
32 Strange South Yorkshire: Myth & Magic in the Valley of the Don
   by David Clarke
33 Collection of Writings About Old Fulwood by Colin Cooper

34 The Mayfield Valley by Muriel Hall & Robert Blackwell

35 More of the Mayfield Valley with Old Fulwood by Muriel Hall

36 A Tree in the Valley by Elizabeth M Perkins

37 Around Bradfield, Loxley & Hillsborough by Malcolm Nunn

38 Penistone by Matthew Young & David Hambleton

39 Woodhouse by Leonard Widdowson & Matthew Young

40 Woodhouse: The Second Selection by Leonard Widdowson

41 Wadesleia to Wadsley by Major CP Kaye

42 A Century of Sheffield 1835 - 1935, Folio One by David Robins

43 The Penistone Scene by RN Brownhill

44 Bygones of Bradfield (Volumes 1 & 2) by Bradfield Local History Group

45 Abbeydale Industrial Hamlet by Sheffield City Museums

46 A Walk Into History by The Dungworth, Storrs & District Local History Group

47 New Light on Old Ecclesfield (supp. 1&2)
    by Ecclesfield WEA Local History Class

48 The Village of Ecclesfield by David Hey

49 A History of Ecclesfield by David Hey

50 Ecclesfield Church, Minster of the Moors - 1500 Years by JM Mayland

51 Ecclesfield Parish: Places & People - A Chapeltown & High Green Archive Publication

52 Yorkshire Memories by David Gerrand

53 Listed Buildings in Sheffield by Barbara A West

54 The Century's Progress - 1893 (magazine article)

55 The Bygone Breweries of Sheffield by David Parry and others

56 Pub Games of England by Timothy Finn

57 Reminiscences of Mosborough 1886 by George Foster

58 The Good Beer Guide edited by Jonathan Preece

59 Sheffield Topic - issues, February, 1984; June & November, 1985

60 Parish Pump - magazine of CAMRA, issue March. 1977

61 Cannon Brewery leaflet

62 Hopcan Gazette - house magazine of William Stones Ltd, No 7, April 1980

63 Sheffield Spectator, issue April 1969

64 Leisure Times - free newspaper, issue June 1990

65 History of Mosborough - pamphlet

66 The definitive A to Z listing of Sheffield Public Houses -
    the final book which I consulted was produced by my friend and
    business colleague, Michael Liversidge

I bid you all goodbye............
There are still pubs out there to record,
but I've written enough and I've said enough.
I therefore willingly pass on that burden to
anyone who wishes to take it up.
For me it is -
"Time, Gentlemen, Please"

Sheffield's paramount purveyor of top quality cask ales
Cask & Cutler

at the centre of real ale excellence in Sheffield

A CAMRA Award Winning Pub

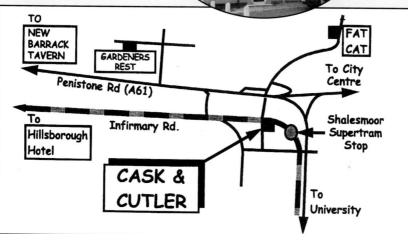

Why not pay us a visit....

- Sensible prices
- Full pints
- No juke box or bandits
- Belgian bottled beers
- Beer garden
- No smoking room
- Selection of Real Ales from independent breweries

Ring Neil or Sheila on 0114 249 2295

Hare &
Hounds

77 Church Street
Stannington, Sheffield 6
telephone: 0114 2341400

**The Village Pub
with something for everyone**

Fine Ales • Great Food • Good Service

Fun Quizzes with cash jackpots

Chess Club • Barbecues